The Rutgers Guide to Lowering Your Cholesterol

A Common-Sense Approach

Hans Fisher / Eugene Boe

RUTGERS UNIVERSITY PRESS
New Brunswick, New Jersey

Library of Congress Cataloging in Publication Data

Fisher, Hans, 1928–
  The Rutgers guide to lowering your cholesterol.

  Includes bibliographies and index.
  1. Low-cholesterol diet.   2. Cholesterol.
3. Nutrition.   4. Low-cholesterol diet—Recipes.
I. Boe, Eugene.   II. Title.   [DNLM: 1. Cholesterol—
popular works.   2. Cholesterol, Dietary—popular
works.   QU 95 F533r]
RM237.75.F57   1985   613.2'8   85–14263
ISBN 0-8135-1135-6

Contents

Part Three: The Rutgers Dietary Approach to Living with Cholesterol

List of Low-Cholesterol Recipes

Acknowledgments

The authors would like to thank Dr. David Otto, Dr. Audrey Burkart, Ms. Nam Soo Lee, Ms. Zury-Lin Hwang, Ms. Dolores Baulis, Ms. Barbara Scott, and Ms. Lori Anne Borselli for their advice and assistance with various aspects of the book. We are also grateful for the expert guidance we received throughout the project from Karen Reeds, Science Editor, Rutgers University Press.

Cautionary Note

The only way to learn your blood cholesterol values—and their significance to your personal health—is to visit your physician and have a blood test to obtain detailed lipoprotein-cholesterol analyses. Because your total cholesterol values may vary greatly from day to day, the tests should be repeated several times over the course of a few weeks to establish your baseline values.

You should discuss your cholesterol levels and other risk factors for coronary heart disease with your doctor and agree on a course of action, including any changes in your diet, that is appropriate for *you*.

The Rutgers Guide to Lowering Your Cholesterol

Introduction

This book was in preparation long before the recent release of research findings that made cholesterol front page news and the subject of national magazine cover stories.

Presiding over a nutrition department in a college or university during the past couple of decades meant being asked about twenty to thirty times a week such questions as:

"Are all these warnings about cholesterol for real?"

"I'm 48 years old and my blood cholesterol is over 300 mg, but my doctor says not to worry about it. Should I worry? Do something to bring it down?"

"If eggs are so loaded with cholesterol, how come people have been eating them since the dawn of mankind and we've never heard that they killed anybody before?"

"Isn't it more heredity than anything else? Like the way you inherit blue eyes or diabetes? Aren't some people just born to have high cholesterol levels?"

"Is anybody saying you absolutely won't have a heart attack if you lower your blood cholesterol?"

"Do I have to give up most of my favorite foods? Like bacon and eggs? Steak? Ice cream? Hard cheeses?"

Enlightened health authorities—including many members of the medical profession—have been answering these questions for quite awhile. They had no need to wait for the recommendations of the National Heart, Lung, and Blood Institute study or of the Consensus Panel convened by the National Institutes of Health in 1984.

For a long time they had been saying that excessive cholesterol must be considered a major risk factor for coronary heart disease.

Since at least the mid-1950s there has been a prevailing impression that cholesterol is "bad" for you, but much confusion and controversy have continued to surround the subject. If it is such a threat, why do some "experts" still claim that "this whole cholesterol business has been blown out of proportion?" Is there necessarily a direct ratio between the amount of cholesterol we consume in our diet and the level of cholesterol in our bloodstream? Granting that cholesterol *is* bad for us, how much of it can we consume before getting into trouble? When it comes down to basics, just what *is* cholesterol?

During the past thirty years or so cholesterol has maintained a rather constant profile. From time to time it has surfaced in the press and broadcast media. A number of scholarly tomes have been devoted to the subject. In many books concerning the health of the heart, the lay public could come upon a few pages or a chapter about cholesterol. There have even been several low-cholesterol cookbooks.

But there has never been a book that really tells the average person all he or she needs to know about cholesterol. This book intends to fill that void. The reader will be brought up to date on all the latest research linking cholesterol with heart attacks. The linkage is irrefutable; anyone who still pooh-poohs the "cholesterol scare" is arguing from either ignorance or vested interest. Some facts will be given strictly for background information, but many will have practical application.

To Gertrude Stein, "A rose is a rose is a rose is a rose." But cholesterol does not submit to such a simplistic identification. There is cholesterol, and there is cholesterol. Within the cholesterol "family" are undesirable members—and a desirable one. There is the difference between cholesterol that is synthesized in our bodies and dietary cholesterol that is part of the food we eat. These important distinctions are made clear in this book.

How can we monitor cholesterol? What are normal levels? What is the cholesterol content in the foods we eat? What else besides food can make a difference?

The key to cholesterol control is now and perhaps forever will be *dietary reform*.

There are some foods we should not be eating so much of and others that are positively beneficial in reducing cholesterol levels. These different foods are specifically identified and enticing menu plans and recipes are provided to encourage the cholesterol-cautious public on its health-seeking way.

But diet will never be the total solution for everybody with a "cholesterol problem." We are only beginning now to appreciate the degree to which exercise, particularly the aerobic kind, can help to lower cholesterol. And there are other factors, expecially the loss of weight.

Some individuals will always have high blood cholesterol levels beyond the corrective powers of a diet-exercise-weight loss regimen. For them, the intervention of medicine is indicated, and various drugs are discussed, with particular benefits and liabilities.

Many of us would do well to modify our lifestyles. We could profitably break some bad habits (especially smoking) and acquire good ones (such as exercise). Above all, we could almost universally dedicate ourselves to eating more healthfully.

A change in lifestyle is *not all that difficult*.

In fact, it is surprisingly easy.

We can go on enjoying, in moderation, most of our favorite foods. Beneficial changes in diet can be achieved quite readily so that no one need feel deprived. For example, if more exercise is advisable, it can be introduced gradually, painlessly, one small step at a time.

A book like this naturally emphasizes prevention. It is always wiser to prevent coronary heart disease—ultimately, heart attacks—than to have to learn how to cope with catastrophe. Prevention, in terms of controlling cholesterol, means first and foremost maintaining vigilance over diet.

In essence, we should heed Thoreau, who believed that a man can consider himself fortunate when his food is also his medicine.

Part One
Defining the Risk

1. The Deadly C-Factor

"Four-egg omelets! My God, a Cholesterol Carnival! Don't they ever want to see any of us again?"
                    —Restaurant customer examining a Sunday Brunch menu

Although it is an essential constituent of our bodies, most of us by now are reasonably convinced of one thing: Cholesterol can be hazardous to our hearts. Often fatally so, particularly among men in their middle years.

We have long known that atherosclerosis, or hardening of the arteries, is the precursor to the coronary heart disease (damage to arteries called "coronary" because they circle the heart) that currently kills 550,000 Americans each year—one person every minute. We have also known that the key to warding off heart attacks is to keep blood vessels from getting clogged with fatty deposits.

For decades, physicians debated: Can too much cholesterol in the bloodstream be blamed for the accumulation of these waxlike build-ups in the tiny coronary vessels? By early 1984, the debate reasonably should have been resolved. All the votes, theoretically, were in. That year, the National Heart, Lung and Blood Institute (NHLBI) announced the results of a comprehensive study to determine whether lowering blood cholesterol could decrease the incidence of heart disease. For more than ten years, 3806 men had been monitored in double-blind investigation (neither the subjects nor the investigators knew who was receiving special treatment). The men were between the ages of 35 and 59 at the outset. All had elevated blood cholesterol levels, above 265 milligrams (mg) per deciliter (a tenth of a liter, or about 3.4 fluid ounces of blood), placing them in the upper 5 percent of the population, but were otherwise judged to be healthy. Half were put on daily doses of cholestyramine, a cholesterol-lowering drug, that was mixed with orange juice. The other half were given a placebo (an inactive substance). Both groups were expected to restrict their consumption of dietary cholesterol to a moderately low 400 mg a day, and the ratio of polyunsaturated to saturated fatty acids was adjusted.

The results of this Coronary Primary Prevention Trial marked a milestone in cardiovascular (heart vessel) disease research.

Basically, the risk of heart attack deaths was found to drop *two* percent for every *one* percent drop in serum blood cholesterol levels. (Blood cholesterol is actually measured in the serum, the clear liquid that remains when the blood is allowed to clot and the clotted solids are removed.) It did not matter whether the cholesterol was lowered by medication alone, by diet alone, by a combination of medication and diet, or by any other means.

The risk of coronary heart disease could be cut in half with dietary reforms, available cholesterol-reducing drugs, or other disciplines.

The link between elevated cholesterol levels and coronary heart disease was irrefutable.

At the end of 1984 the National Institutes of Health (NIH) went the NHLBI study one further. Its Consensus Panel of distinguished physicians and scientists reported that high blood cholesterol levels were a direct cause of heart disease, not just an associated risk factor. Quite certainly, thousands upon thousands of lives could be saved every year with a frontal attack upon cholesterol alone.

Central to the panel's advice was that we stop thinking of "average" as "normal." For example, in the United States middle-aged adults have cholesterol levels that average 200 to 230 mg (the deciliter is implied and usually omitted from descriptions). That is too high. It is desirable that anyone over the age of 30 have a cholesterol reading of 200 mg or less. Levels above 220 mg place the individual in moderate-to-high risk. We should consider as normal what is best for the health of our hearts, the panel advised.

Population studies throughout the world have demonstrated

that people with blood cholesterol levels below 150 mg almost never develop heart disease. While cholesterol among Americans tends to rise with age, atherosclerosis is not inevitable with advancing years. For instance, heart disease is rare among old people in Japan, Greece, and in almost all non-Westernized countries where the diet is very low in total fats and especially low in saturated fats and cholesterol. (See Part One, Chapter 3 for description of fats.)

In his landmark Seven Nations Study initiated in 1947, Ancel Keys of the University of Minnesota found direct correlations between a country's incidence of heart disease and the amount of fat in the national diet. The Finns, with the fattiest diet, had the highest cholesterol levels and the highest rate of heart disease. The Americans, with a diet only slightly less rich, were a close second. The Japanese, who traditionally ate a diet low in fat, had the lowest cholesterol levels and the least cardiovascular disease; their rate of heart attacks was *one-fourth that of Americans.*

The future health of Japanese coronary arteries is a matter for grim conjecture. While the average cholesterol level in Japan is now only about 190 mg, it is 20 mg higher than it used to be before prosperity led to the consumption of more meat. Such fast-food emporiums as McDonald's, Kentucky Fried Chicken, and David's Cookies have recently found an enthusiastic welcome in Japan, a development likely to be reflected in further rises in blood cholesterol. In one revealing study, Japanese men living in Hawaii were found to be considerably more susceptible to heart attacks after being introduced to a semi-Westernized diet, and the number of fatalities rose sharply among Japanese men who emigrated to the continental United States.

Beginning in 1957, and continuing for the next twenty years, Western Electric in Chicago studied 5400 of its male employees in the 40–55 age bracket. Diet information was obtained and coded by nutritionists. Serum cholesterol was elevated in workers whose consumption of saturated, or animal, fats was high; it was lower when polyunsaturated fatty acids, or vegetable oils, were prominent in the diet. The Western Electric observers came to the conclusion that dietary cholesterol was significantly associated with the risk of death from coronary disease.

But it was the famous Framingham Heart Study—the most

comprehensive project of its kind in medical history, begun in 1949 and still continuing—that deserves credit for first bringing cholesterol to the consciousness of the general public. Some 5000 men and women were followed over many years. The first report, issued in 1957, strongly suggested that cholesterol levels in the bloodstream bore a pronounced relationship to the subsequent development of coronary heart disease. (The Framingham Study, incidentally, is purely observational and does not involve counseling.)

In the beginning, the Framingham Study did not investigate the effect of changing these levels through diet or other means. Later, dietary histories were taken, and the consumption of animal fat and total dietary cholesterol were examined. Subjects were then warned to eat fewer eggs, the greatest single source of cholesterol in the diet.

Dr. William P. Castelli, director of the Framingham Study, stated that "cholesterol seems to be the keystone" in producing heart disease. When blood cholesterol is low in a general population, studies show there is little or no heart disease even if high blood pressure and smoking are prevalent.

The higher the cholesterol level, the higher the risk. An adult with a cholesterol level of 240 mg is two times more likely to suffer a heart attack than an individual with a count of 200 mg. "Doctors may not believe this is a cause-and-effect relationship," Dr. Castelli recently observed in an interview with the *New York Times*, "but if they're smart, they'll act as if it were." They will advise their patients about dietary reforms, exercise, losing weight, and other factors that can help to reduce blood cholesterol.

Early fatalities from heart disease are not exclusively a phenomenon of recent times. For millennia, man's heart has been failing prematurely. Clogged arteries were found in an Egyptian mummy dating from about 100 B.C. In his *Dell'Anatomia*, written in the late fifteenth century, Leonardo da Vinci pinpointed atherosclerosis as the cause of a "slow death without any fever." With a disease whose progression may be as silent as it is slow, we can only speculate on the number of people throughout history—famous and otherwise—whose exact cause of death went undetected.

Many pathologists have long maintained that aging of the human body starts with the blood vessels, which, in societies like ours, become increasingly harder as we grow older. Moreover, this action takes place before other organs begin to show signs of age. The way to keep the body young, then, must be to prevent blood vessels from thickening and hardening with fatty deposits.

Although people have suffered and died from coronary heart disease through recorded time, the term "heart attack" was not coined until 1896. Medical researchers in the present century, once the condition was named and described, began to look for the underlying causes. They examined the coronary arteries of heart attack victims and found them as brittle as old pipes and clogged with deposits of cholesterol. Cholesterol, they came to suspect, must be a prime factor.

It is therefore plain that cholesterol levels should be lowered. Moreover, as the scientific community has gradually realized, cholesterol levels *can* be lowered. The process of atherosclerosis is stoppable, possibly even reversible. The current epidemic of cardiovascular disease conceivably might go the way of the epidemics of infectious disease—smallpox, diphtheria, scarlet fever, measles, influenza, pneumonia, tuberculosis, polio—that were the big cripplers and killers early in this century.

The number of risk factors that have been associated with heart disease by one source or another is nearly astronomical.

The Cardiology Division of the University of Utah Medical Center in Salt Lake City has assembled a list of no fewer than 246 such factors. These cut a wide swath, including race, climate, altitude, noise levels, divorce, feelings of loneliness, church attendance, possession of an automobile, hyperthyroidism, gout, diverticulitis, gallstones and kidney stones, vasectomies, deficiencies of magnesium, potassium, manganese, copper, vitamins B, E, and C, and a host of other nutrients, as well as a low consumption of onion, garlic, and yogurt.

During the past fifty years medical science has identified the following as likely to signal an increased chance of developing atherosclerosis:

- Age
- Gender (male)
- Genetic makeup (heart disease, strokes, and heart attacks in near relatives)
- Abnormal electrocardiogram

- Environmental stresses
- Hypertension (high blood pressure)
- Cigarette smoking
- Personality and behavior ("Type A" personality)
- Lack of physical activity
- Use of alcohol (but moderate drinking may actually *reduce* the risk)
- Use of drugs (oral contraceptive pills)
- High blood uric acid
- High levels of lipids in the blood
- Cholesterol
- Triglycerides (another fatty substance)
- Fatty acids and phospholipids
- Lipoproteins (fats attached to proteins)
- High blood insulin
- Diet
    - High caloric intake
    - High fat intake (especially saturated fat and insufficient polyunsaturated fat)
    - High cholesterol intake
    - High sucrose intake
    - High or low intake of certain minerals
    - Soft drinking water
    - High coffee intake
    - Nutrient deficiencies
- Presence of other disease
    - Diabetes mellitus
    - Gout
    - Obstructive liver disease
    - Hypothyroidism
    - Nephrosis
    - Pancreatitis

But the road to a fatal heart attack is strewn with a specific set of *most* dangerous factors:

- High blood cholesterol levels
- Elevated blood pressure

- Smoking
- Obesity
- Stress
- Lack of exercise
- Alcohol or drug abuse
- Personality type
- Heredity
- Aging

We all grow older. Besides aging, the only major risk factor that would seem to be beyond our control is heredity. But even here there is room for encouragement. Unfortunate genes may be a predisposition to high jeopardy for heart disease, the current thinking goes, but judicious habits may deny those genes the opportunity to express themselves and may postpone, for an indeterminate time, the date of a genetically likely heart attack.

Of the major risk factors, the three most formidable are: high cholesterol levels, elevated blood pressure, and smoking.

The greatest threat may well be too much cholesterol in the bloodstream.

Heart attacks have been called Public Enemy Number One. They are responsible for more deaths in the United States than any other disease and rank second in cumulative hospitalization time only to all forms of cancer combined.

In addition to the more than half million of us who will die from heart attacks within the year, another 680,000 will be hospitalized by them. Some 5.5 million of us have been diagnosed as having cardiovascular disease, and many others of us do not know we have it.

The direct cost of cardiovascular disease is $8 billion per year, and the total cost (including all the nonmedical ramifications of an ailing heart) is $60 billion. Coronary bypass surgery, which detours blood around the clogged portion of the artery, is the most common heart operation. It is a $3 billion industry and costs the average patient about $30,000. Heart transplants fetch up to $250,000. An artificial (bionic) heart is a multimillion-dollar investment.

The simple truth is that much of this pain, expense, and aggravation is avoidable.

Do you know this man?

He is such a familiar fellow that we will give him the name of Joe Smith.

Joe lives in an apartment down the hall, in the house next door, or no further away than a block or two up the street. He is 47 years old. If he could keep just one of his New Year's resolutions, it would be to take off twenty-five pounds.

Yes, Joe has heard all the warnings about cholesterol. But his preferred way of getting a good start on the day is a couple of fried eggs (sunny side up), two strips of bacon, and a slice or two of buttered white toast. After breakfast he drives from the suburbs downtown to his quite stressful job as regional sales manager for a firm manufacturing personal computers.

More days than not, Joe must take people to lunch. As host, he will order a round or two of drinks. He will recommend the most expensive entrees on the menu (Delmonico steaks or roast prime ribs of beef). The wine will flow freely. For dessert there may be a butterscotch sundae or a slice of hot apple pie topped with a slab of cheddar cheese.

The tensions of the day may have got Joe smoking more than a pack of cigarettes. It would be a good idea, he'd agree, if he went from work to a swim, a jog, or a bit of tennis or squash. But it's late. He wants to catch the evening TV news. He looks forward to dinner with his family, a meal that usually includes red meat as a main dish. After dinner Joe will watch some TV. To relieve the tedium, he will anesthetize himself with a few cans of beer and a package of potato chips. Joe's wife finally prevails upon him to have that long-deferred physical examination. He learns, among other things, that his blood cholesterol is dangerously high. He must make some drastic changes in his lifestyle, or else.

Joe Smith has a lot of company. As a nation, our diet does not appear to have been planned in any way. And it certainly does not protect against disease.

The food we eat reflects our affluence, our technology, our productive agriculture, our abundant meat supply, our responses to advertising, our growing tendency to crave convenience foods and meals-in-a-jiffy, our ethnic "taste," and a multiplicity of other influences not based on nutrition or good health practices.

But by now most of us are well aware of the principal foods that boost cholesterol counts: egg yolks, fatty meat, and dairy products. We know that a diet rich in these foods can be the starting point for the slow degenerative process that thickens the arteries, hinders the flow of blood, and leads to an unnecessarily early death.

For more than a decade, the American Heart Association and other health organizations have been urging Americans to lower their blood cholesterol levels by reducing their appetite for fatty, cholesterol-rich foods. Also, the American Medical Association (AMA) has been recommending cholesterol-lowering diets for people with so-called normal levels. But until the release of the NHLBI findings in 1984, it had yet to be demonstrated conclusively that reducing cholesterol levels for a period of years can actually lower the risk of heart attacks.

Public awareness of the cholesterol threat *has* changed behavior. Since 1963 the average American cholesterol intake has dropped from up to 800 mg per day to less than 500 mg. The consumption of fluid milk and cream has declined by 24 percent, butter by 33 percent, eggs by 12 percent, and animals fats by almost 40 percent (thanks in part to the breeding of leaner beef and pork). At the same time, the consumption of vegetable oils and fats has risen 60 percent.

The NIH panel advised that the fat content in our diet should be limited to no more than 30 percent of the total calories. Saturated fats should be kept under 10 percent, and the proportion of polyunsaturated fats should be increased. Today we are still consuming the same proportion of total fat (about 43 percent of the calories in our diet) that we were a decade ago. We may have cut back on steak and butter only to take up the fat slack with too much fried chicken, french fries, and other fast-food favorites.

Still, many of our changing eating patterns are all to the good, and implicit in these is the growing acceptance of the message: *Saturated fats and cholesterol can be killers.*

This year one out of five American males will have a heart attack before the age of 50, but only one out of seventeen women will.

The discrepancy between the danger to men and to women accounts for the reputation of cardiovascular disease as the special scourge of middle-aged men.

Almost everybody, girls as well as boys, has low cholesterol levels at birth. But at puberty, boys experience a 20–30 percent drop in the "good" kind of cholesterol, linked to protective, high-density lipoproteins (HDLs). (See Part One, Chapter 3 for details on HDLs.) Race may also be a factor; changes in boys at puberty are more pronounced among whites than blacks.

"It is almost as if white males are genetically programmed for early coronary disease," Dr. Gerald Berenson, director of an extended heart study in Bogalusa, Louisiana, has commented.

Premenopausal women enjoy a virtual immunity to this malady. (See Part Two, Chapter 6.) Sex hormones also have a considerable impact. Estrogen increases HDLs, and testosterone (male sex hormone) lowers them. But estrogen given to men has not been effective; men have suffered impotence, developed larger breasts, and become "restless, dissatisfied and depressed."

The strength of the protective factor in women is impressive; even premenopausal women from a family background of high cholesterol levels appear to be protected. After their mid-fifties, however, women face a risk of death from heart disease approximately equal to that of men, and the parallel continues into old age. Women and men alike with high levels of cholesterol, associated with low-density lipoproteins (LDLs), have an increased heart disease risk into the seventh and eighth decades of life.

The American Medical Association and others rightly urge that blood lipids (cholesterol and other fatty substances) should be measured at or before the age of twenty—particularly for males. Recently, other authorities have suggested this should be done at puberty. Young men in their twenties with a blood cholesterol count even slightly over 200 mg are probably at undue risk for coronary disease in the future.

The Korean War offered some sobering data on the young. Autopsies were performed on many American, Chinese, and Korean soldiers. The average age of the American casualties was only twenty-two, but more than 35 percent of them already displayed the early stages of developing atherosclerosis. *No* fatty arterial deposits whatsoever were found among the other soldiers. The difference: the Asian troops had been raised on a diet of rice and vegetables. It is a cruel irony that where famine is rife and meat is rarely seen cardiovascular disease is almost unknown.

Why do high levels of cholesterol in the blood lead to heart disease? A common explanation is the injury theory. The disease begins when the thin protective layer of cells (endothelium) that lines the arteries becomes damaged. This damage can result from high blood pressure (which forces blood against the artery wall with extraordinary power), from the insult of cigarettes, and possibly from viral infections and other causes.

Normally, injury to a healthy artery lining is swiftly repaired, but not after the onset of atherosclerosis. Too much cholesterol, high blood pressure, or smoking apparently interferes with the normal healing process. So starts the insidious descent into decay and destruction.

What sets off this potentially fatal process is a complex exchange of signals among various types of cells that gather at the scene of injury. First to arrive may be small blood cells called platelets, normally associated with clotting. The platelets emit chemical signals that somehow cause smooth muscle cells—usually confined between the endothelium and the outer layer of the artery—to find their way to the damaged area. There they multiply quickly to produce a mesh of elastic fibers and connective tissue.

Macrophages, large white cells in the vessel wall that become free during injury or inflammation to gobble up foreign particles, contribute to the chaos by rushing in and filling up with cholesterol from the blood. This conglomeration of cells becomes engorged, bursts, and releases its cholesterol. More white cells arrive to "clean up" the debris. These, in turn, become distended and also explode. And so it goes. The accumulating mass forms a patch, called plaque, resembling a lumpy scar.

When cholesterol levels in the blood are reduced by any means, the plaque may not only cease to grow but may even shrink. But if people, particularly men, persist in bad habits year after year, the plaque grows progressively larger. Ultimately, the flow of blood may become seriously obstructed.

The contrast between the sick and the well could not be sharper. In healthy persons, the blood flows through arteries as freely and naturally as water in a babbling brook. In people with plaque-laden arteries, the flow is disturbed and diminished.

If the damaged vessel is a coronary artery, an individual will probably first experience the warning signal of chest pains. If the artery becomes completely clogged, a heart attack will result. If the blocked artery is one that usually supplies blood to the brain, the result will be a stroke. For as many as one-third of the victims of atherosclerosis—either by heart attacks or by strokes—*the first manifestation of disease is instant death.*

Cholesterol is a molecule found in every cell in the body. It is present in large amounts in nerve tissues and in the brain; and also appears in the skin, the adrenal glands, and the liver. It does not contribute to the energy derived from food but is needed by the body for a number of functions. It is a main ingredient in the fatty sheath that insulates the nerves, an important part of sex hormones, and the major constituent of bile and an enzyme that helps to digest fat. (See Part One, Chapter 3 for more details.)

It is ironic that an essential constituent of body tissues can also be deadly. How does this happen? The liver produces 800–1000 mg of cholesterol every day, 70–80 percent of the cholesterol circulating in the bodies of most individuals. The healthy body has its own mechanism for regulating cholesterol levels. It can reduce the amount produced by the liver and slow the pace at which it is absorbed. It can also turn more of the cholesterol into bile.

But if we eat so much cholesterol that our bodies cannot deal with it effectively, blood cholesterol levels rise. For some 10–15 percent of the population the body's cholesterol-regulating mechanisms are mildly to severely deficient because of genetic factors. These people, above all others, *must* keep their consumption of dietary cholesterol very low.

Blood cholesterol in different individuals on the same diet may range from below 150 mg to extremely high levels. Some people will always be able to eat anything and stay out of danger; others, however they diet, will remain cholesterol-high; a third group is intermediate. Different mechanisms appear to underlie the varying levels of blood cholesterol in a normal population.

No responsible authority can say that limiting the intake of dietary cholesterol to 300 mg a day—or even less—will prevent coronary heart disease in everybody. Nor would cardiovascular disease completely disappear if everyone were to eliminate saturated fats and to stop eating eggs, butter, and meat altogether. There will still be those who require sophisticated treatment for other risk factors.

In the twenty or more years that researchers have been seriously exploring the role of cholesterol in the development of heart and cardiovascular diseases, they have identified thirteen lipoproteins—substances containing fat and protein—that circulate in the blood in cholesterol-containing complexes. Only five of these lipoproteins are generally identified as being of paramount importance.

Using lipoprotein levels as a guide—particularly LDLs—medicine hopes to be able to treat patients long before they develop irreversible symptoms of the hardening of the arteries that leads to heart attacks. A simple fingerpricking screening test for cholesterol levels may be available within a year or so, Dr. Antonio Gotto, president of the American Heart Association, has indicated. Such a test could be used in airports, schools, and shopping malls on large numbers of people to detect those who may be at risk and who should make immediate changes in their lifestyle.

For many with dangerously clogged coronary arteries, the only available relief has been the costly surrender to coronary bypass surgery; a vein is removed from the leg and used to create a detour around a blocked artery.

Now there is hope for a technique called laser coronary angioplasty that might someday clean out clogged arteries without recourse to surgery. A laser, emitting an intense light beam, attached to flexible glass fibers encased in a thin tube called a catheter can be threaded through arteries to reach—and obliterate—plaque. But the technique has not yet been tried on living patients, and any widespread employment is years away.

Prevention, the catchword in health care these days, is a more immediately applicable measure.

The best way to reduce the chances of heart attacks is to adopt preventive measures early and to keep risk factors in abeyance.

Twenty years ago we Americans took a fatalistic attitude toward heart attacks. If you got one, you got one. Heart attacks were neither predictable nor preventable.

We no longer think this way. We know that in general our health is in our own hands. We know in particular how much we ourselves can do to protect the health of our hearts. Above all, we are coming to know—and accept—the bad news about cholesterol.

If we are all becoming so cholesterol-conscious, the question arises, "Why do we need another book on the subject?" The answer is that, to the best of our knowledge, no comprehensive book on cholesterol addressed to the general public has yet been published.

Many people may feel that having heard the word so often—usually in a pejorative context—they know as much as they need to know about the subject. They know cholesterol is bad for the heart. But knowing this is not the same as having precise, usable information.

If something so directly affects the health of the heart, as cholesterol does, it is prudent to learn everything we can about it. Only when armed with all the facts can we adjust our habits and decisions to conform with what is best for us.

The good news, we now know, is that cholesterol is largely controllable. We can bring menacing levels down through dietary reforms, exercise, and other easy-to-implement modifications in lifestyle. (In extreme cases, medication may be necessary.) This book aims to provide all the available data needed for understanding and coping with a potent but manageable threat to the human heart.

2. Not Only in America

"Sure, pork is loaded with cholesterol, but look at the bright side—
no caffeine."

—Butcher to customer in the cartoon strip, *The Better Half*

Coronary heart disease may be labeled *the* malady of the twentieth century, but it is American men in their middle years who are most likely to suffer sudden, fatal heart attacks. With the rarest of exceptions, however, the risk factor of high blood cholesterol in the development of atherosclerosis is as universal as it is democratic.

Historically, coronary heart disease has been much more common in Western countries than in the Far East. In mainland China, Taiwan, Japan, and Korea the incidence has been very, very low. In southern Japan, for example, in the years immediately following the end of the Second World War, 10,000 autopsies disclosed that the incidence of severe coronary atherosclerosis was only a tiny fraction of that observed among persons of the same age in Minnesota.

In China, a low-fat diet and the absence of smoking were considered factors in protecting the people from heart attacks. But the people of the Kirghiz steppe in Central Asia, with a diet quite high in animal fat, were very prone to hardening of the arteries. Also, Japanese in Hawaii and the mainland United States, as noted earlier, have become more susceptible to coronary heart disease as their diet has become more Westernized. Simply being of Oriental extraction, then, confers no immunity.

As early as 1916, a Dutch physician, C. D. De Langen, published a report based on years of practice in Java. He found that the Javanese had much lower levels of blood cholesterol than did most Dutch citizens living in the Netherlands; moreover, they had less atherosclerosis, phlebothrombosis (solid masses, such as clots, in the veins), and gallstones. He might have been inclined to assume that these differences reflected ethnic or racial peculiarities, but he also observed that Javanese crews who ate Dutch food on Dutch passenger ships had blood cholesterol levels similar to those of his fellow countrymen.

Dr. De Langen began recommending the indigenous, low-cholesterol Javanese diet, largely rice, other vegetables, and fish, as good preventive medicine. Over a period of five years, in the 500-bed municipal hospital in Djakarta, he discovered only one case of angina pectoris (chest pain due to an inadequate blood supply to the heart) among the Javanese and six cases among Chinese patients. But among Dutchmen and Chinese in Java who ate rich European food, coronary heart disease was commonplace.

When Yemenite Jews began migrating to the new state of Israel, they had much lower blood cholesterol and less coronary heart disease than did Jewish settlers from Europe. Researchers initially looked for a racial or genetic explanation. In time, studies showed that the Yemenite Jews were gradually losing their comparative invulnerability as they became acclimated to Israel and adopted the dietary habits of European Jews. Dietary fat, blood cholesterol, and coronary heart disease all increased.

In 3000 autopsies on Bantu and Eurafrican patients in Johannesburg, South Africa, in 1946, only two cases of coronary thrombosis (masses or clots in heart blood vessels) were found. Again a racial trait was suspected, but a closer look revealed that the patients' diets were very low in fat and cholesterol. Subsequent long-term dietary experiments involving both Caucasian and Bantu prisoners showed no appreciable difference in cholesterol levels when the two races ate the same diet.

In the United States, race has also been proposed to explain differences in susceptibility to heart disease. For a time it was claimed that the Navajo Indians of the Southwest ate a typically American diet but rarely developed coronary heart disease. However, the Navajo diet, upon analysis, proved to be anything but "typically American." Instead of getting more than 40 percent of their calories from fat—the average for the U.S. population—the Navajos' fat consumption was only one-fourth of their daily caloric intake. Their meat consumption was minimal, and four out of five ate butter less than twice a week. Another Indian tribe, the Tarahumaras of New Mexico, who have remarkably low cholesterol levels, also have a low dietary intake of both cholesterol and saturated fats, and about 96 percent of their protein comes from vegetable sources, compared with only one-third for most Americans.

Early Eskimo populations, noted blubber and meat eaters, also were singled out as people who disprove a relationship between fat consumption, cholesterol levels, and the incidence of coronary heart disease. But few such Eskimos lived long enough to reach the age when coronary heart disease is most common. Arctic explorer Vilhjalmar Stefansson rhapsodized over the Eskimo's healthy subsistence on a diet of seal meat. But these reports were impressionistic and not based on medical examinations or reliable statistics. A year-long medical study of Eskimos in northern Greenland revealed that arteriosclerosis was very common. The traditional Eskimo diet, as a matter of fact, disappeared over fifty years ago with the introduction of white flour and sugar as staple foodstuffs throughout the Arctic. Furthermore, this diet had been fatty only during the sealing season but quite low in fat during the fishing season.

With the exception of the Masai tribe of East Africa, no controlled dietary experiments have disclosed any racial or population discrepancies in the universal relationship between dietary fat and blood cholesterol. Japanese coal miners whose diet, during a research study, uncharacteristically contained butter did not differ in their blood cholesterol response from a group of men in the dairy state of Minnesota, whose diet habitually included butter. If low blood cholesterol is associated with certain countries—for example, Italy, Spain, Greece, and Guatemala—it is because those countries have diets relatively low in saturated fats.

The Puerto Rico Heart Health Program and the Honolulu Heart Study, undertaken concurrently in the 1960s, involved some 8200 and 7200 men, respectively. In both studies the subjects who consumed more starch were less likely to develop coronary heart disease or have fatal heart attacks, and the assumption was that they were also consuming less fat than the other subjects who did not fare so well. (The decrease of starch consumption in the United States has gone hand in hand with the increase of coronary heart disease—and presumably with the rising consumption of animal fats.)

Diets low in total fat will necessarily be low in saturated fats. Some diets can be high in total fat, it must be emphasized, but low in saturated fats; the saturated fat content has the most relevance to blood cholesterol. Diets in rural Greece, for instance, are usually high in total fats, but these are mostly olive oil (monounsaturated) so that blood cholesterol remains quite low. The liberal use of olive oil, but minimal amounts of other fat, also characterizes the cuisine of Italy and Spain; the result, similarly, is a high-fat diet low in saturated fat. Very recent research suggests that the monounsaturated fatty acids found predominantly in olive oil may be as beneficial, if not more so, than the polyunsaturated oils.

The Second World War and the years before and after it provide instructive data on the link between health and diet. Very early into the war, Finland became victim to the severe restriction of some foods, notably fats. But the general level of health held up astonishingly well. There was a baffling decrease in the incidence of coronary heart disease and in the severity of atherosclerosis observed at autopsies.

The Nazi occupation brought similar food privation to Norway. Within two years the mortality rate from coronary heart disease fell sharply and remained low until after the end of the war when imports began to relieve the food shortage. Sweden, Denmark, and the Netherlands also reported fewer heart attacks with dietary reduction in fats.

England, however, was another story; it suffered severe food rationing but only a small decrease in the per capita supply of fats. It experienced only a small drop in coronary heart disease mortality. In the United States the per capita consumption of fats actually rose during the war years, and there was a steady increase in deaths attributed to cardiovascular disease.

German prisoners of war in the Soviet Union during World War II were put on stringent rations containing only 8 percent fat and showed no evidence of coronary artery disease. In Germany itself during the postwar years of occupation, while food deprivation continued there was hardly a case of coronary heart disease or a heart attack victim to demonstrate to medical students.

Routine autopsies in Graz, Austria, showed that from 1935 to 1970 heart attacks rose 1000 percent, far more than any other disease. But during the war years of 1939 to 1945, when *Schlag* (heavy cream) and other cholesterol-rich foods were not available, heart attacks dropped by 75 percent. (During the war years, however, there were many deaths from tuberculosis.)

In all of embattled Europe the war years brought a drop in total calories as well as a decrease in dietary fats. Chocolate, tobacco, and coffee—all suspected of having a deleterious effect on the heart—became scarce. Civilians worked unusually long hours, burning up more energy and perhaps trimming down to their optimum weight for the first time in years. The accompanying decline in mortality from coronary heart disease probably involved *all* the most important causes, but the lower death rate during these "lean" years began to rise again in the late 1940s as soon as life once more became "easier."

The inference is inescapable: dietary restrictions and other sacrifices imposed by the war were basically *healthy*; were they to prevail in peace time, the incidence of coronary heart disease might be permanently lowered.

In 1981, *Lancet*, the British medical journal, published the results of research on a group of Oslo men between the ages of 40 and 49 who were at high risk for heart attacks. These Norwegians had cholesterol levels ranging from 290 mg to 380 mg. All smoked. Their blood pressure was in the upper quartile (fourth) of the population. Some of the men were given a change of diet to decrease their blood lipids and were asked to cut down on smoking. They were rewarded with rates of heart attack (fatal and nonfatal) and sudden death 47 percent lower than for men who did not modify their eating and smoking habits. The researchers concluded that the benefits to the subjects derived mainly from the change in diet.

A year later *The New England Journal of Medicine* reported on a study of the population of North Karelia, a county of Finland, where the rate of coronary heart disease was high and high blood cholesterol was prevalent. In a group of middle-aged men put on a low-fat diet that contained a high ratio of polyunsaturated to saturated fats, the total blood cholesterol decreased significantly.

Also in Finland, the mortality from coronary heart disease and other causes was studied in two Helsinki mental hospitals during a 12-year controlled or preventive trial. The patients in one hospital were put on a cholesterol-lowering diet; the patients in the other hospital continued to eat the regular hospital fare. After six years, the diets were reversed, and the experiment was continued for six more years. Among the men, the cholesterol-lowering diet significantly correlated with reduced deaths from coronary heart disease (also with lower mortality from other causes). Differences among the women were not so statistically significant because there were too few heart fatalities during the period of the managed diet. Nevertheless, the change to a cholesterol-lowering diet from the usual hospital food decreased the death rate from coronary heart disease by about half, and a return to the "normal" hospital diet more than doubled the death rate.

The diet of the Israelis was scientifically examined over a 28-year period, from 1949 to 1977. During that time the Jewish population in Israel increased from 1,175,000 to 3,493,000. It was an era of rapid technological, economic, and health advances. Food production, life expectancy, and the use of electrical appliances increased, while infant mortality decreased to 17.8 per 1000 live births.

But at the same time per capita caloric consumption jumped by 16 percent, fats by 52 percent, and protein by 16 percent, parallelling an increase in the consumption of meat by 454 percent, sugar by 52 percent, dairy products by 18 percent, and vegetable oils by 53 percent. The use of wheat products *decreased* by 22 percent and of fish by 49 percent. During those years the mortality from heart disease rose from 101 deaths per 100,000 males in the 1950–1954 period to 345 per 100,000 in 1977. Heart disease became far and away the major cause of death (43 percent) followed by cancer (18 percent). All investigated mortality rates bore a significant positive association with the increasing total consumption of fat.

Over a period of three and a half years, groups of older European Jews in Israel were matched against Yemenite immigrants. The European groups had far higher cholesterol levels and a correspondingly higher rate of atherosclerotic heart disease.

Even in the Soviet Union, which is hardly known for its consumer abundances, cardiologists are said to be alarmed by increasing heart attacks—even among young persons. Smoking and excessive avoirdupois are prevalent, with some 40 percent of the male population visibly overweight.

The habitual diets of Polynesians living on the islands of Pukapuka and Tokelau are high in saturated fat but low in cholesterol and sucrose (cane or beet sugar). Coconut, whose fat is saturated, is the chief source of energy for both groups of islanders, 63 percent of the food supply for Tokelauans and 34 percent for the Pukapukas. Despite this high intake of saturated fat, especially by the Tokelauans, blood vessel disease is uncommon in both populations, perhaps because coconuts have no cholesterol and the rest of the islanders' diets is so low in cholesterol.

The Maoris, another Polynesian people, have lived for centuries in New Zealand, where their lifestyle has changed dramatically compared to that of Polynesians who have remained in more isolated South Pacific environments. This probably explains the Maoris' relatively high rate of mortality from cardiovascular disease. An 11-year inquiry into the deaths of Maori men between the ages of 25 and 74, as reported in the *British Medical Journal*, divided the fatalities into three categories: cancer, cardiovascular disease, and "other." About one-third were from coronary heart disease and one-third from cancer. Curiously, the deaths from heart disease could not be correlated with high blood cholesterol and might reflect more the generally poor nutrition of an underprivileged group living in a Western industrial population.

Two other racially identical Polynesian groups revealed unusual dietary differences. The Rarotongans, who had come under considerable European influence, consumed substantially more calories and protein than did the Atiu-Mitiero Islanders. But the traditional island diet contained saturated coconut fats twelve times in excess of such fats in the Rarotongan diet. Males 40 years or older had significant differences in body build and blood pressure. The Europeanized Rarotongans were more overweight, had higher blood pressure in general, and had a higher incidence of excessively high blood pressure. However, the Atiu-Mitiero men, though living a simpler, more traditional Polynesian life as planter-fishermen, had cholesterol levels higher than the Rarotongans, presumably because of the abundance of saturated fats in their diets.

Most developing countries report a continually rising incidence of heart disease and fatal heart attacks. The picture is darkening even for some countries that seemed to benefit from fortunate dietary customs. For example, in Japan, as early as the 1960s—and to a much greater extent in recent years—diets steadily increased in fat content and in the proportion of fat derived from animal sources. This change coincided with the more frequent appearance of advanced stages of atherosclerosis.

China, historically blessed with what may be the healthiest cuisine in the world, has been virtually free from deaths brought on by cardiovascular disease. But cholesterol levels among some men are increasing, associated with a gradually rising incidence of coronary heart disease. The average blood cholesterol levels, according to a recent study, are 136 mg for normal men and 190 mg for cardiovascular patients, and those levels are still dramatically lower than those of comparable groups in the United States. It is a safe assumption that a growing taste for Western-style foods accounts for the rising cholesterol levels.

Reports of increasing coronary heart disease in recent years in so many parts of the globe probably also reflect greater recognition of the malady through better diagnosis. Nevertheless, its near-universality earns this disease its reputation as "the epidemic of our time."

3. The Cholesterol Family: Bad Members—And the Good One

Mother is being served breakfast in bed on Mother's Day. She hears the sputtering of eggs frying in bacon fat and wonders if she is the intended victim of a Cholesterol-Nitrites Conspiracy.

—Columnist Russell Baker

What exactly is cholesterol?

Corner a biochemist in his laboratory, put the question to him, and he may respond, "It is a member of the cyclopentano-perhydrophenanthrene family, whose particular designation is 3-hydroxy-5,6-cholestene."

Now that *that's* perfectly clear . . .

In our minds we associate cholesterol with saturated or animal fats and assume that it too is a fat. Actually, in its pure state, it looks and feels somewhat like liquid soap. Technically speaking, it is an alcohol—specifically a sterol, or complex solid alcohol. Its molecule, containing 25 carbon atoms, is relatively large, which contributes to the waxiness of most of the fat-cholesterol deposits in arteries.

As mentioned earlier, cholesterol is needed metabolically. However, it is not an essential element of diet. The human liver and other tissues (intestine) can manufacture it from glucose or fatty acids at the rate of perhaps 50,000,000,000,000,000 molecules per

second, or about 1 gram per day in a normal person. Thus, cholesterol can be made by the body from either carbohydrate or fat, even
if foods contain no cholesterol at all.

The cholesterol molecule is not an unusual type. Among the
many similar ones are bile acids, sex hormones (e.g., testosterone),
adrenal hormones (cortisone), and vitamin D.

After its manufacture, cholesterol either leaves the parent tissue
or is transformed into related compounds such as the sex or adrenal
hormones. Cholesterol that leaves the liver may join the bile and
move into the intestine to be partially excreted in the feces and partially reabsorbed into the blood from which it may be taken up by
body tissues or deposited in arteries.

Some of the cholesterol made by the liver and other tissues is
converted in the liver into bile salts which are secreted through the
bile into the intestine where they help to emulsify fat. About 90 percent of these bile salts return, carrying absorbed products of fat digestion, in a kind of recycling merry-go-round. They go back to the
liver, join newly made bile salts, make their way back into the intestine, and once again emerge and head toward the liver to complete
another cycle.

In the intestine, however, some of the bile salts can be am-
bushed by certain kinds of dietary fiber (pectin) or drugs (cholestyramine), which expel them from the intestine with feces. This
excretion of bile salts causes more cholesterol in the liver to be converted to bile salts and thus reduces the total amount of cholesterol
remaining in the body. Excretion of cholesterol in the feces in the
form of cholesterol itself or as bile salts is the only major route for
cholesterol removal from the body.

Some cholesterol from the liver enters the blood in combination with other fats (cholesterol and various fats are members of a
chemical family called lipids) and other nutrients—protein and carbohydrate—that subsequently find their way to the body tissues.
These water-soluble packages of blood proteins, carbohydrates, and
lipids, including cholesterol, are called the lipoproteins. Without the
protein and carbohydrate portions of the lipoprotein complex, the
cholesterol and other fats can no more dissolve in the blood than
grease can dissolve in water. The blood transports the lipoproteins

through the arteries, into the capillaries, and to the body tissues, which then extract lipids, including cholesterol. Lipids are an important concentrated source of energy for the body.

The lipoproteins have been likened to floating tankers in the blood, carrying lipid fuel to the cells. An enzyme in the capillaries that service fat cells and muscle cells makes the energy accessible.

More than nine-tenths of all the body's cholesterol is located in body cells rather than in the blood serum (the clear, watery component of blood). It is in the cells that it performs its essential structural and metabolic functions. But for cholesterol to reach the cells, lipids must first pass through the artery walls, and this is where they may become involved in artery disease.

In the blood, there are five different kinds of lipoproteins that transport cholesterol. The three most important are:

Low density lipoprotein (LDL)

Very low density lipoprotein (VLDL)

High density lipoprotein (HDL)

(The names reflect differences in the ratio of protein to fat. The more protein in a lipoprotein, the greater the density and the smaller the particle size. In the laboratory, the various lipoproteins can be separated by their densities. There is much ongoing research into further subdivisions of the five categories of lipoprotein.)

A fourth lipoprotein, and the largest in particle or droplet size, is the chylomicron, derived exclusively from the absorption of dietary fat in the intestines. Although they contain cholesterol, chylomicrons carry mostly triglyceride (a form of fat) and very little protein, perhaps only 1 percent, in contrast to HDL which is as much as 60 percent protein. The protein in lipoproteins is usually referred to as apoprotein.

VLDL is the other major carrier of triglycerides (the triglyceride and VLDL blood levels are strongly related). VLDL also plays an important role in the risk of developing cholesterol deposits in blood vessels. The lipid portion of VLDL is, in part, incorporated from dietary fats, but the major portion is synthesized in the liver for the transport of triglycerides to other tissues of the body.

The LDL particle is smaller than the VLDL particle and different in composition. Unlike the chylomicrons and VLDL, which are largely made up of triglycerides, LDL is predominantly cholesterol and phospholipids (lipids containing phosphorus). Furthermore, LDL has proportionally more protein than either VLDL or HDL. LDL represents a residue or by-product of VLDL metabolism; VLDL becomes LDL after giving up a portion of its triglyceride to various body tissues including the liver.

The LDLs are the chief villains suspected of causing major cholesterol deposits. They are the "baddest guy" in the cholesterol family. In normal, healthy individuals, LDL enters the cells of the body through specific receptor sites on the cell surface. Inside the cell, enzymes separate the cholesterol from LDL, and the action of free cholesterol influences the rate of new cholesterol synthesis, particularly in the liver. The more free cholesterol in the cells, the less new synthesis. However, in people who have a hereditary condition known as familial hypercholesterolemia, a genetic defect sharply reduces the number or efficiency of LDL receptor sites, much less LDL gets into the cells, and less cholesterol is freed. The reduction of free cholesterol reduces the inhibition of cholesterol synthesis so cholesterol production is abnormally high.

HDL, in contrast to LDL, is formed and released by both the intestine and the liver. HDLs have smaller particles than any of the other lipoproteins. They are the "good guys" because they have the ability to pick up cholesterol from nonliver tissues and from other lipoproteins. They carry it back to the liver where it can be converted to bile salts and/or directly eliminated through the bile. Cholesterol returned to the liver by HDL may also reenter the blood as part of newly synthesized VLDL. Because cholesterol deposition in the arteries is linked to the accumulation of cholesterol in cells, HDL apparently helps to prevent this by removing such accumulations. The cholesterol thus removed from the cells by HDL is converted into cholesteryl esters. These esters, which are combinations of cholesterol with fatty acids, are embedded inside the core of the HDLs and transported to the liver for potential excretion through the bile.

High HDL levels have been associated with families in which succeeding generations live to be 80 or 90 years or older without developing gross cardiovascular disease. For people without a lucky

heredity, HDL levels can be raised to some extent by dietary reforms, exercise, sex hormones (estrogen, in particular), and small
amounts of alcohol (though this may give rise to other problems).
Obesity and smoking are factors which appear to *reduce* HDL.

While the liver and intestine manufacture much of the body's
cholesterol, an additional source of potentially troublesome cholesterol, and fat, is the food we eat. To be circulated by the blood to
body tissues, both fat and cholesterol must first be digested—
mostly in the small intestine.

The fat is largely in the form of triglycerides. Because triglyceride particles are too large to be absorbed across the intestinal wall,
they are broken down to smaller particles (glycerol, fatty acids, and
some monoglycerides) by enzymes secreted by the pancreas. Once
these products of triglyceride digestion are absorbed into the intestinal cells, the triglycerides reform and are packaged into chylomicron particles. The chylomicrons pass through the intestinal wall
into the lymphatic system (an auxiliary circulation similar to blood
but without blood cells), where they begin to appear within three to
four hours after fat has been consumed, then enter the venous system near the heart and join other fats in the blood. As they circulate,
much of the triglycerides in these lipoproteins are taken up by
adipose (fat), heart, and muscle tissues. The remaining lipoprotein
is taken up and degraded by the liver.

The life of the chylomicrons is less than an hour following their
absorption.

Cholesterol from food absorbed in the intestine, together with
cholesterol newly synthesized in intestinal cells, is linked with long-
chain (large molecule) fatty acids to form substances called cholesteryl esters, and incorporated into chylomicrons and VLDL in
the intestinal cells. In contrast with the rapid turnover and equilibra-
tion of dietary triglycerides, dietary cholesterol comes into balance
with blood cholesterol only after several days, and may take several
weeks to reach an equilibrium with other body tissues. Free cholesterol is formed when the chylomicron remnants, after giving up
their triglycerides, are taken up by the liver. Free cholesterol in the
liver and blood reaches an equilibrium level much faster than cholesterol locked into chylomicron and VLDL, usually within only a
few hours.

Over the short term, days or weeks, blood cholesterol levels remain relatively constant regardless of fluctuations in dietary intake or physical activity. In the long term, months and years, these levels can change considerably. Regrettably, they often escalate.

The discovery of cholesterol is attributed to Michel Eugene Chevreul of France. Even before Chevreul, De Fourcroy argued in 1789 that the crystalline substance obtained from human gallstones was the same as spermaceti (oil obtained from sperm whale and used in cosmetics) and was related to what he called *"adipocire"* ("fatty wax"). But other observers experimenting with this substance found that it remained unchanged after boiling with potassium hydroxide and that its melting point differed from those of both spermaceti and "adipocire."

In 1816 Chevreul introduced the designation *cholesterine*, taken from the Greek *chole*, meaning bile, and *steros*, meaning solid. Cholesterine was found in human bile by Chevreul in 1824 and somewhat later in human blood and in the brain by Lacanu and Couerbe, respectively. Lacanu is also credited with its discovery in hens' eggs.

In the succeeding decades cholesterine was gradually recognized as a normal constituent of all animal cells and various secretions, as well as a component of certain pathological deposits. When it was discovered, at the beginning of the twentieth century, that cholesterine was chemically an alcohol, its name was changed to cholesterol to reflect this new information. Its complete chemical structure was finally worked out in 1932.

The intimate connection between cholesterol and fats is well recognized.

Fats, often called lipids, are actually a family of compounds that includes both fats and oils. They provide a concentrated form of energy and contribute to body health. Natural oils in the skin enhance complexion, help lubricate the scalp, and give the hair its gloss. Fatty tissues protect body organs from heat, cold, and mechanical shock, and insure a continuous energy supply. Fats act as a solvent for the fat-soluble vitamins and the many compounds that give foods their flavor and aroma. A pad of fat beneath each kidney protects it from being jarred and damaged, safeguards it even from the bumps of pothole-ridden city streets. Similarly, the soft fat in the breasts of a woman cushions them against shock, as well as providing the mammary glands with a shield against heat and cold.

What exactly are fats, or lipids?

Start with glycerides. A glyceride is a combination of glycerol (derived from glucose sugar) and fatty acids; one fatty acid makes a monoglyceride, two fatty acids a diglyceride, and three a triglyceride. Most of food and body fat is in the form of triglycerides. A blood triglyceride measurement reflects the amount of fat in the serum (cell-free blood liquid). The recent Consensus Conference on Hypertriglyceridemia suggested that levels below 150 mg/dl should be disregarded.

The terms saturated, monounsaturated, unsaturated, and polyunsaturated have to do with the chemical structure of the fatty acid component of the fat. Fatty acids are chains of carbon atoms that may be short (e.g., the four-carbon chain of butyric acid, found in butter) or long (e.g., the 18-carbon chain of linoleic acid, found in most vegetable oils). The carbon atoms have sites for the attachment of hydrogen atoms which may or may not be filled. If all are filled with hydrogen, the fatty acid is said to be saturated. Saturated fatty acids tend to make a fat solid at room temperature, but there are exceptions. Some short carbon chain saturated fatty acids are liquid, notably the butryic acid that occurs in butter. Unsaturated fatty acids have vacant hydrogen positions on two adjacent carbon atoms. A fatty acid with one vacancy is called monounsaturated; two or more vacancies make the acid polyunsaturated.

The most common polyunsaturated fatty acid is linoleic acid, found in most vegetable and cereal fats. Although linoleic acid is needed for normal metabolism and is thus considered an essential fatty acid, the body is unable to synthesize it. Another essential fatty acid, perhaps metabolically the most important one, is arachidonic acid. It is found primarily in fish oils (cod liver, sardine, and herring) and can be synthesized in the body from linoleic acid. Arachidonic acid serves as the precursor for the hormone-like prostaglandins that have many important regulatory roles in the body.

There is some evidence that another fatty acid, linolenic acid, which the body cannot make from either linoleic or arachidonic acid, is also an essential fatty acid. Symptoms of a deficiency of essential fatty acids include dermatitis (skin inflammation), more frequent infection and dehydration, and liver abnormalities.

Plant fats, in general, are rich in polyunsaturated fatty acids. Most fats derived from nonvegetable sources, e.g., animal fats, are rich in saturated and low in polyunsaturated fatty acid. Some exceptions are chicken fat, which is generally not as saturated as beef fat, and fish fats (or oils), which are often highly polyunsaturated. Coconut and palm kernel oils and cocoa butter, plant fats, are highly saturated and not at all similar to the common seed and cereal oils. Unfortunately, coconut and palm oils are commonly used in processed foods, particularly the "better" margarines. Although their effects on health may differ, animal and plant fats have nearly equal caloric value.

The consumption of a diet rich in saturated fats but poor in polyunsaturated fats will for many, though not all, individuals *increase*, detrimentally, the concentrations of LDLs and the total cholesterol in the blood.

Plant foods are completely free of cholesterol. Among the polyunsaturated, cholesterol-lowering oils are those derived from corn, soybean, sesame seed, cottonseed, sunflower seeds and safflower seeds. Between the desirable polyunsaturated fats and the harmful saturated fats are fats such as olive and peanut oils, which are relatively rich in monounsaturated fatty acids. Until recently these were believed to be neutral in effect, but are now thought to be as effective as the polyunsaturated fats in lowering LDLs without reducing the level of the HDLs.

Fats, in a word, are complicated. For example, polyunsaturated fats vary in degree of polyunsaturation; linoleic acid has two vacancies (four hydrogens missing) while fish oils may have as many as five or six. Also, a specific food need not have exclusively one kind of fatty acid or another. Of the three fatty acids that make up a triglyceride, two may be saturated and one polyunsaturated, or one may be saturated, one monounsaturated, and one polyunsaturated—any combination of the three is possible.

Most animal fat is rich in saturated fatty acids but may also contain others. Fatty acids in beef fat, for instance, are about half saturated and just under half monounsaturated; some two percent are polyunsaturated. Chicken, on the other hand, is relatively low in total fat but contains roughly the same amounts of saturated and polyunsaturated and somewhat more of monounsaturated fatty acids. Much of the fat is concentrated in the skin. Chicken fat and human milk fat can be changed and made more polyunsaturated by giving the chicken or a nursing mother a diet low in saturated fat (animal fat) and rich in polyunsaturates (vegetable oils).

Highly saturated fats are hard at room temperature; less saturated ones are soft or liquid. Beef fat, accordingly, is visibly more saturated than chicken fat. Butterfat is more saturated than some margarines and solid vegetable shortenings. Most vegetable oils are unsaturated unless they have been deliberately hydrogenated in processing to produce a hard fat like shortening.

Regardless of the quantity and nature of fat intake, how rapidly deposits of cholesterol build up may to a large degree depend on genetic predisposition. Genetically, some people are "hyperresponders" and some "hypo-responders" to dietary cholesterol. As Dr. Henry Blackburn, of the University of Minnesota's School of Public Health, has observed, "Genetic susceptibility determines the individual's risk of atherosclerosis and diet explains the population's risk."

Through the millennia, there have no doubt always been some people genetically susceptible to atherosclerosis, but the danger was small as long as diets were based mainly on foods like grains and vegetables, and infectious diseases were likely to cause death at ages before atherosclerosis would manifest itself. It was only in this century, when Western populations began overloading their diets with animal fats, and when antibiotics, vaccines, and public health measures sharply reduced mortality from other causes, that genetic defects made themselves known through an epidemic of atherosclerosis and heart attacks.

It is our view that some people and groups seem to be genetically programmed to escape the perils of extra dietary cholesterol. The Pima Indians of Arizona are an example. They have the world's highest known incidence of diabetes and one of the highest incidences of obesity. Their diet is heavy in foods fried in lard. Yet they have moderately depressed levels of LDLs and only about one-fourth as many heart attacks as the general American public. It has been surmised that their bodies produce as much cholesterol as do other peoples' but are more efficient at removing it from their bloodstreams possibly because the LDL receptors on their cells are more numerous or more efficient. Such enhanced receptors promote the entry of LDL into tissue cells where the cholesterol burden is detached, thus removing cholesterol from the bloodstream and producing free cholesterol whose presence inhibits the production of new cholesterol. The receptors can be considered crucial components of a cholesterol disposal system. Scientists have recently suggested that this surmise may apply to many other people who are untroubled by cholesterol build-up.

The number of LDL receptors may be increased by cholesterol-lowering drugs. It is possible that further investigation of this lipoprotein transport system may be the key to an understanding of just how genes, diet, and hormones interact to regulate blood cholesterol levels in man.

The Masai, a nomadic tribe of East Africa, are another people apparently unthreatened by cholesterol. Their diet consists almost entirely of cow's milk, small amounts of meat, and a little blood. Yet, despite a fare so full of saturated fatty acids, they have low cholesterol levels, low blood pressure, and little coronary heart disease.

There are mitigating factors. The Masai men are extremely lean and athletic and do not smoke. They are chronically underfed and frequently half-starved. The milk they drink often sours in the tropical heat, which may have special effects.

But the Masai probably also have a very effective feedback mechanism, genetically determined, to suppress cholesterol synthesis by the body. Even a Westernized Masai, after ten years of living in the United States, showed the same pattern of low total cholesterol and lipoprotein levels as his fellow tribesmen. (Curiously, another tribe of nomads in East Africa, the camel-herding Rendille, whose diet is almost exclusively camel's milk, do not have low cholesterol values.)

Maybe no more than one or two percent of Americans, according to a Rockefeller University geneticist, have a genetic composition that makes them immune to atherosclerosis. Such immunity has been called the Winston Churchill Syndrome. Presumably people in this fortunate group could break all the rules and live to be 90, eating bacon, eggs, and buttered toast for every breakfast, lunching on quiches or cheese omelettes and ice cream sundaes, dining on well-marbled steaks with baked potatoes and sour cream, and smoking and drinking prodigiously. But how many Sir Winstons are there among us? And who, on top of a heedless diet, would dare to lie abed all day consuming two quarts of brandy and smoking a dozen or more cigars?

At the other end of the spectrum, about one in 500 Americans may be genetically deficient in LDL receptors, will develop dangerously high levels of LDLs, and have twenty-five times the normal risk of heart disease.

In a family known to us, with such a predisposition, the father and one brother (a physician) died of heart disease by age 50. A younger brother, determined to beat the odds, retired from business in his forties, was careful about diet and exercise, and is now 76.

There can be no gainsaying that blood cholesterol levels are an important index in predicting the danger of heart attacks and strokes, particularly for men under 50. But the index is not infallible. Some people with low cholesterol *do* develop clogged arteries, and others with elevated levels show no signs of it.

This apparent paradox can be explained, certainly in part, by our growing comprehension of the blessing of HDLs. An individual with a low total cholesterol level but also a very low HDL level may still develop cholesterol deposits. Conversely, someone with a high cholesterol level but who has a high HDL level may not be at any significant risk for a heart attack. Low HDL may be inconsequential for individuals who also have low LDL levels.

The standard total serum cholesterol measurement includes the cholesterol present in both LDLs and HDLs. The ratio of HDL to total cholesterol may be as important, if not more so, than the total cholesterol count by itself.

If that ratio is less than 1 part HDL to 4.5 parts total cholesterol, some authorities suggest that treatment is indicated. Conceivably a relatively low 200 mg of total cholesterol combined with a low HDL level of, say 35 mg (a ratio of 1 "good" part to 5.7 "bad" parts) might indicate a typical candidate for heart disease. Fortunately, it is often possible to improve the ratio by changes in eating patterns, exercise, and behavior. We can welcome the "good" members of the cholesterol family and discourage the black sheep.

4. Cholesterol: The Diminishing Controversy

"I'm off to the delicatessen for some fried cholesterol. But what a way to go."

—Night club comedian greeting a friend on Broadway

The institutional guardians of our health have been anything but reticent in their warnings about dietary cholesterol. In recent years their voices, in response to mounting evidence, have become even more cautionary.

Since 1980, the United States Departments of Agriculture and Health and Human Services have been publishing a brochure urging the public to avoid too much cholesterol and fat, especially saturated fat. Officials of both departments have been meeting with scientists to discuss whether or not this warning should be more stringent and specific.

These departments now have the NHLBI findings and the recommendations of the NIH Consensus Panel to underscore their concern.

For many years, the American Heart Association has been advising people to limit themselves to 300 mg of cholesterol a day (roughly the amount contained in a single egg). (See Appendix, Tables 1 and 2, for cholesterol content of common foods.) The Council on Scientific Affairs of the AMA, after reviewing the literature on diet in the prevention and treatment of coronary heart disease, concluded that the "average total plasma cholesterol levels of 180 to 220 mg/dl . . . seem to be associated with a low incidence of both cardiovascular and other diseases and probably should be considered optimal."

All of this notwithstanding, the nay-sayers are still among us:

"That whole cholesterol business has been blown way out of proportion."

"Personally, I don't go along with any of it. Been eatin' what I like all these years and I'm still here."

"If you ask me, the jury's still out on this one."

There are even doctors today who still claim to be less than convinced. Cholesterol is only the best of the "lousy indicators," they sneer. Protesting their aversion to "cholesterophobia," they ask why the whole country needs to be put on a low-cholesterol diet. Does it make any more sense than having everybody taking insulin out of fear of diabetes? In short, they argue, it is time to bury "with full military honors" the cholesterol theory.

It is always interesting, and often instructive, to hear out arguments that seem to tilt against the weight of overwhelming documentation. But when we look carefully at these arguments against taking cholesterol seriously, we find they are flawed, and it is important to understand how they are flawed. Sometimes they are simply old, discredited arguments that should have long ago been consigned to oblivion. Sometimes it is important to question the source of the criticisms and the possible motives of the critics.

Some contend that the number of heart attacks—like Mark Twain's reported death while he was still in his prime—has been greatly exaggerated. They point out that any sudden, unexplained death not due to the blocking of one or more coronary arteries is *not* a heart attack. But, in the absence of an autopsy, such a death is usually signed out as a "heart attack" by the family physician. Thus, it is claimed, the actual number of heart attacks could be less than one-third the recorded number.

This seems to be vastly overstating the case. Nowadays it is unusual for someone to keel over and die without some hint of the real cause. Testing machinery has become widely available and increasingly sensitive to detecting heart irregularities and frailties.

The high proportion of deaths from cardiovascular disease,

another argument goes, must be viewed in relation to changes that
have occurred in the general state of health. Statistics are at the
ready: Since 1900 the mortality rate in the United States has fallen
from 17 to less than 9 per 1000 persons; infant, childhood, and ma-
ternal mortalities have fallen to one-eighth, one-twentieth, and one-
thirtieth, respectively, of their levels in 1900–1910. So what if the
world's highest death rates from coronary heart disease are found in
the United States and the Northern European countries? Aren't these
the very countries—Sweden, Norway, Denmark, the Netherlands,
Switzerland, the United States, and Canada—in which life expectancy is greatest? Anyway, we all "gotta go sometime." True, we all
"gotta go sometime," but better later than earlier, which we can
hope for if we can maintain ourselves in reasonably good health.

Statistics may be accurate as far as they go, but ultimately misleading. The final questions may not get asked. How much greater
might our life expectancy be, for instance, if people (particularly
men of a certain age) were not being cut down prematurely by many
self-imposed factors? Also, we surely want to make our older years
as comfortable and independent as possible. We must not forget that
heart disease, strokes, and atherosclerosis disable many more people
than they kill.

In June 1983, *Nutrition Today* declared that two documents
might well "shape the health professions and other affected groups
such as the food activists, the vegetable oil industry, the publications industry, the health food faddists, and others" in much the way
that "the two volcanic eruptions in southwestern Washington sent
tremors through that state and caused fallout of extensive proportions elsewhere." The two documents were *Toward Healthful Diets*
and the *Hulley Report*.

Toward Healthful Diets, in fact, appeared one day after the first
dramatic eruption of Mount St. Helens in the state of Washington.
Published by the National Academy of Sciences' Food and Nutrition
Board, it concluded, in part, "It does not seem prudent at this time
to recommend an increase in the dietary [polyunsaturated to saturated fat] ratio except for individuals in high-risk categories. . . .
The fat content of the diet should be adjusted [by the physician] to a
level appropriate for the calorie requirement of the individual." Dietary fat intake, in other words, is a concern not of a public health

project but of the practicing physician. The Board offered no specific recommendations covering dietary cholesterol.

In 1980 the Board could be excused for not having the benefit
of the latest results of so many studies and trials—the Framingham
Heart Study and the NHLBI Study foremost among them.

Published also in 1980, the *Hulley Report*—the work of University of California (San Francisco) epidemiologists—discussed
the "frailty" of the assumption that eating foods containing triglycerides is hazardous. While conceding that the "evidence surround-
ing the hypothesis that serum cholesterol is a cause of coronary
heart disease is broad and consistent," the Report declared the theory about the dangers of triglycerides to be "wounded gravely, perhaps mortally."

The Hulley Report's emphasis on triglycerides was misin-
formed. The trouble area has been and continues to be the cholesterol and saturated fat content of the food we eat.

"If the millions spent trying to prove the cholesterol bug-a-boo
had been spent on studies of the enzymes responsible for elevated
blood cholesterol and causes of the initial lesions, etc.," opined
Milton L. Scott, Professor Emeritus of Poultry Nutrition, Cornell
University, "we might already have saved many, many lives that have
been lost to heart disease."

Professor Scott's criticism is beside the point. While research
into the causes of the injury to blood vessels and into enzymatic
mechanisms involved in cholesterol metabolism is clearly desirable,
it should not displace the research that has demonstrated just how
risky high cholesterol levels can be. By alerting people to the dangers of cholesterol and teaching them ways to control their cholesterol, the research rejected by Professor Scott has saved many
lives.

Dissenters quote the Surgeon General's Report of 1979 declar-
ing that the population of the United States has never been healthier.
"Is it prudent to change our present diet without hard evidence at a
time when our life expectancy has reached 73 years," inquired Robert M. Kark, M.D., at Presbyterian-St. Lukes Hospital in Chicago,
"and the incidence of myocardial infarction is rapidly declining?"

"Never been healthier" describes a present—not a possibly at-
tainable and better—condition; the health of tens of millions could

be improved by altering harmful habits. Yes, Dr. Kark, it is prudent to change our present diet. Life expectancy could keep rising while the incidence of heart attacks continued to decline, and the quality of life could be significantly enhanced.

Some nutritional associations maintain that the American food supply is generally wholesome and provides adequate quantities of nutrients to protect all healthy Americans from deficiencies. This is undoubtedly true, but availability of food does not guarantee judicious choices. If we are so well-fed, we might ask, why is obesity (actually a form of malnutrition) so prevalent? Well, we are told, this only reflects the Disneyland of appetizing foods our country offers.

Admittedly so. But as recently as February 1985 the NIH warned us that *obesity is a killer.* Furthermore, obesity should be regarded as *20 percent* above ideal weight, not 40 percent as previously defined.

"Galileo would have flinched if he had observed the pseudo-scientific procedures of the American Heart Association regarding the cholesterol 'propaganda,'" wrote Dr. George V. Mann of Vanderbilt University's School of Medicine in the *New England Journal of Medicine* in 1977. Scientific issues are being settled by majority vote, he charged, dietary research is becoming busywork for thousands of chemists, and to be a dissenter is to be unfunded because the peer review system rewards conformity and excludes criticism.

But that was 1977. In the interim there have been too many long-term, carefully controlled studies on cholesterol for such charges of bias to be creditable. The American Heart Association merely happened to be in the avant garde in its warnings.

Other skeptics are heard from:

The amount of calories and cholesterol in red meat is far lower than commonly perceived by the public, maintains the Director of Research and Nutrition Information of the National Live Stock and Meat Board. He also alleges that many consumers are not aware of the positive contributions of meat to diet, such as protein quality, vitamins, and minerals. (The pork industry, nothing if not adaptable, has become defensive about "fat" and uses the punning phrase "lean on pork" in its advertising, and the meat industry in general has been moving toward the promotion of leaner cuts of meat and reducing the fat content of meats.)

The president and general manager of a large food company's agricultural products division, speaking at an American Feed Manufacturers Association annual convention, grants that high levels of cholesterol in the blood can be dangerous to health but insists that red meat is not a cholesterol problem today in the diet of Americans.

We are also warned not to eat too much polyunsaturated fat—some of the compounds formed from the breakdown of such fats (for example, by heat) might be toxic to the body because these compounds have apparently caused cancer when injected into or fed to animals.

These various objections boil down to much ado about not very much. Not even the staunchest advocates of reduced cholesterol consumption advise that red meat be completely eliminated from the diet, nor do they dispute its nutritional merits. Nor do they promote the unlimited intake of polyunsaturated fats. The best advice, harking back to the wisdom of the Greeks of antiquity, is: Everything in moderation; too much even of a good thing can create problems.

The "opposition" also points out that the body can synthesize 90 percent of the cholesterol it uses, irrespective of dietary intake. Because blood cholesterol varies independently of dietary cholesterol, dietary cholesterol is *not* the principal element that controls the level in the blood. Limiting dietary cholesterol to 300 mg or less per day would help some people, but others in need of more "sophisticated" treatment would be given a false sense of security. If margarine and substitutes for eggs and meats are recommended, they should be urged on the merits of taste, physical qualities, and price, not as medicines.

Reasonable people would not necessarily disagree with any of these contentions. Yes, the body can make much or most of the cholesterol it uses. Yes, other factors than diet enter into blood cholesterol levels. Yes, drastic reductions in dietary cholesterol would not meet the needs of all who are at risk for cardiovascular disease. Yes, too, any substitutions for foods high in cholesterol or saturated fat should be adopted because they are acceptable as food and not because they have the aura of being medicinal.

Reasonable people would still point to the findings of recent research as a reminder to the wise. Perhaps *all* of us ought to keep some watch on our intake of cholesterol and saturated fat.

The release of the findings of the decade-long research conducted under the auspices of the NHLBI has only given fresh ammunition to some of the doubting Thomases.

The periodical *Feedstuffs* charged that some officials and physicians were guilty of an "overzealous interpretation" of the study's results. To be fair, *Feedstuffs* conceded, the NHBLI study at least demonstrated the apparent effect of one anticholesterol drug. So classify it as a drug, not a nutritional, study.

The drug cholestyramine was chosen for the study, *Nutrition Today* remarked, because it substantially lowers cholesterol by reducing low-density lipoproteins, but as far as diet is concerned, the study proved only that dietary modification alone has a minimal effect on lowering the risk of heart disease. An eminent statistician interviewed by *Science* took the study to task for including only subjects with abnormally high levels of blood cholesterol. (It is worth noting that he did find the comparisons of diets and rates of heart disease in various populations persuasive reasons for limiting cholesterol intake).

These and other detractors make points of dubious value. True, the subjects in the NHBLI study all had abnormally high levels of blood cholesterol. But who better to lend themselves to such a trial; who in compassionate terms would have been more in need of effective intervention? When cholesterol is very elevated, diet alone admittedly will not reduce lipid levels enough to remove risk. But neither will any drug by itself ever obviate the need for a close, unremitting watch on diet.

There is simply no rationalizing away the powerful impact of dietary cholesterol and saturated fat on hearts in jeopardy. The question is whether proper dietary restrictions can have a counteractive positive impact.

Dr. Richard A. Kunin, author of *Mega-Nutrition* holds (rightly) that low-fat diets in themselves are not sufficient to prevent atherosclerosis.

To buttress his conviction, Dr. Kunin cites 10,000 autopsies performed at Dachau that revealed the presence of atherosclerosis in blood vessels. These starving concentration camp victims consumed at most a low-fat diet of a thousand calories a day and exercised strenuously at hard labor while they were alive. They must have been deficient in nutrient components that counter atherosclerosis, he concludes. But may it not have been that the atherosclerotic build-up was formed in the years when the victims were free and eating diets probably quite high in cholesterol and saturated fats?

Low blood cholesterol may not necessarily be an indicator of good health, other nutritionists warn. They say it might be a sign of advanced malnutrition or even starvation. According to proponents of a system called orthomolecular therapy, deficiencies of vitamins C and E and other micronutrients are among the most important causes of atherosclerosis and coronary heart disease. These vitamins are said to protect against free radical damage to cells in blood vessels. (Free radicals are highly active, electrified chemical fragments that can injure the nucleus of cells if not trapped by compounds such as vitamin E.)

Others offer similar comments:

"I have a strong impression," writes Dr. Roger J. Williams, discoverer of pantothenic acid (a B vitamin), "that if we get into our systems a good assortment of essential nutrients, the matter of cholesterol, saturated fats and unsaturated fats will pretty much take care of itself."

"Although it is widely known that animals fed diets high in cholesterol and saturated fats will develop atherosclerosis," declares Dr. Carl Pfeiffer, "the same is not true for human beings if adequate amounts of other nutrients, such as zinc and chromium and vitamin C, are ingested."

There are those advocates of megavitamins who claim that massive amounts of vitamin C (up to 15 g—grams—a day) partially remove plaque from arteries in the majority of coronary patients. They further claim that the gradual drop in coronary heart disease in recent years can be attributed to the increasing use of megadoses of the vitamin—as sales of vitamin C have gone up, they allege, the rate of coronary heart disease has come down.

These claims and suppositions are suspect. For example, increasing sales of vitamin C do not mean that people in any great numbers are consuming it in megadoses; more people may be using vitamin C but in moderate amounts of, say, 500 mg a day in the hope of warding off colds. Nor can there be much disagreement with health authorities who contend that most people would not be bothered with cholesterol worries if they ate a truly prudent diet.

Some who dispute the cholesterol risk appeal to other sorts of arguments:

Any severe change of diet would wreak havoc on the employment and income of millions of people involved directly or indirectly in agriculture. This is a page borrowed from the propaganda of the tobacco industry, which bewailed the plight of poor tobacco farmers who would be deprived of their sole source of livelihood if cigarette advertising were banned or, worse, if everybody stopped smoking.

Agriculture is undeniably having difficulties. But American farmers have always shown pragmatism and flexibility—if one commodity was no longer in demand or another became desirable, they rose to the challenge.

"Cholesterol levels of most people not affected by food eaten, Missouri study finds." That is how *Poultry Times* headlined a report on a recent University of Missouri study. A closer look at the study teaches skepticism about the *Poultry Times* story. The diet of a group of male medical students was controlled for two three-month periods, each period culminating in stressful final exams. Half the students abstained from eggs during the first period then ate two eggs a day during the second period. The other half ate two eggs a day during the first period and abstained during the second. The aim of the study was to see whether the stress of final exams had any influence on serum cholesterol. In fact, the stress did not seem to affect cholesterol levels, but giving up eggs significantly lowered them—a finding *Poultry Times* glossed over.

Another argument is that dietary modifications late in life—especially after clinical appearance of coronary heart disease—will probably not change invalidism and mortality. Even if coronary patients welcome dietary restrictions—it gives them something to do, holds out some hope of improving their prospects, and is better, psychologically, than being told there is nothing they can do beyond quitting smoking—it's pretty much locking the stable after the horse has fled.

This is definitely not so. All evidence suggests that, as people grow old, atherosclerotic plaque continues to grow. It is always advisable to lower blood cholesterol, and blood pressure, at any age.

The cholesterol controversy may not be laid completely to rest soon. Specialists speaking out from various corners, sometimes perhaps self-servingly, will continue to discount cholesterol as a major risk factor for heart disease or deny any "meaningful relationship" between blood cholesterol and cholesterol and saturated fats in the diet. But it seems safe to predict that their numbers will diminish and that their contrary statements will fall on less receptive ears.

A strong clue to the way the wind is blowing came out of the NIH Consensus Development Conference on Lowering Blood Cholesterol, held in December 1984. *Science* reported the observations of Dr. Daniel Steinberg, Chairman of the Conference: "The *real* news was . . . the remarkable *consensus*. The panel reached its conclusions unanimously, and, on the basis of what we heard during the 3-day conference, both from the speakers and during the extensive discussions from the floor, there were not more than a handful among some 600 conferees who appeared to disagree with the general terms of the recommendations."

The overwhelming consensus was that high blood cholesterol is one cause of coronary artery disease. Further, any cholesterol level above 240 mg should be treated aggressively by at least dietary means. They agreed, in other words, that almost one-fourth of the U.S. population should take decisive action to reduce a recognized risk factor for heart attacks.

Part Two
Toward Cholesterol Control

1. How Cholesterol-Conscious Are We . . . Really?

"Why is Santa's face red, Daddy?"
"He's probably been drinking too much."
"How come he's so fat?"
"Maybe all that junk food and cholesterol rolling around in his belly."
—Conversation overheard in a department store

Ask almost anyone what cholesterol is. You may not get a definition that satisfies a biochemist, but chances are the answer will show that the very word cholesterol has become disreputable and almost synonymous with a "no-no."

The proverbial "man in the street" also knows in a general way which foods are cholesterol-rich.

He may even be able to tell you not only his blood cholesterol level but the ratio of his HDLs to total serum cholesterol.

If he has a "cholesterol problem," he knows he should be making major changes in his diet.

Like the man in the street, most of us give at least lip homage to "good nutrition." We are increasingly aware of the crucial role that eating prudently plays in enhancing our health and well-being, as well as in staving off deterioration, disease, and premature death.

And yet . . . there is that lingering inconsistency between knowing which foods are good for us, which are bad, and actually eating mostly the good.

"Consumers are telling us loud and clear what they want," declares a spokesman for a food conglomerate that manufactures bread products, frozen dinners, and soups. "Fewer additives, less salt, sugar, fat and cholesterol. Plus convenience." Indeed, in the marketplace we can now find canned vegetables and tomato juice without added salt, unsweetened canned fruits, whole grain breads and cereals, low-fat dairy products, high-protein pasta, and low-sodium potato chips, pretzels, and club soda. Mineral and spring waters, "lite" beers and wine are "in," and orders for cocktails and highballs are fewer.

Meat, egg, and butter consumption is down. The demand is for leaner meats; beef and pork are being bred to be less fatty. Poultry and fish are increasingly popular, and more people are discovering meat substitutes. Consumers are also turning to salads abundant with exotic greens, sprouts, fennel, chick peas, snow pea pods, yellow pepper, and red onions.

However, the fast-food dynasties continue to dispense fatty hamburgers, hot dogs, barbecued ribs, fried fish and chicken, and french fries in the millions. Some of them, bowing to trendiness, have salad bars, but among the most popular ingredients are bacon bits, shredded cheddar chese, cubed ham, fried croutons, cole slaw, and potato salad (often thickly coated with mayonnaise), all topped perhaps with a thick Roquefort cheese dressing.

Quiches, omelets, soufflés, and mousses are still going strong. One of the most "in" desserts is crème brûlée (a standard recipe calls for eight egg yolks and one quart of heavy cream).

Rushed, pressured urbanites breakfast on juice, a "danish" or doughnuts, and coffee. Or on packaged cereals that are sometimes more sugar than whole grain.

But the Standard American Breakfast is still eggs and bacon (or ham or sausages) and buttered white toast. Should anyone doubt this, let him travel the breadth of the continent and observe what people eat for their first meal of the day in hotel and motel restaurants, small town cafes, the fast-food chains, or their own homes. Pancakes—the other early morning staple—come with lots of empty calories in white flour and sugar (maple syrup) and with plenty of cholesterol and fats (eggs in the batter and melted butter with the syrup). Oatmeal, the healthiest of breakfast foods, is virtually a no-show.

Egg substitutes (totally cholesterol-free), now available every-where, are not commonly used in the ubiquitous quiches, omelets, and soufflés. Nor are they in the sauces of the "nouvelle cuisine" that rely so heavily on egg yolks.

Croissants, one of the food rages of the 1980s, are 60 percent fat, in terms of calories, in contrast to the 5–10 percent in regular breads and rolls. The growing cornucopia of convenience foods in-cludes "deluxe" TV dinners, almost half of whose calories are in fat, and frozen vegetables in pastry, which are 55–65 percent fat.

There may be a rising demand for low-fat milk, yogurt, and cottage cheese and for diet margarine, but, according to the Depart-ment of Agriculture, we are eating more hard cheese—calorically three-quarters fat—than ever before. Most cheeses have more fat—and more calories—ounce for ounce than red meat.

We are also in the midst of an "ice cream explosion" (is there anyone in the world with taste buds so jaded or perverse he can hon-estly say he does not like ice cream?). And the brands of ice cream most fancied are the pricier, "creamier" ones that have almost twice as much fat as the cheaper brands in supermarket freezers.

Restaurateurs catering to affluent and sophisticated clienteles report that poultry and fish are in high favor—but so are rich des-serts, even when a sugar substitute is used in the coffee. "At the end of the meal," as one put it, "diners feel they deserve a reward for having been so 'good.'"

Chicken nuggets are now the "hottest" thing on the fast-food circuit. Any switch away from red meats (burgers, hot dogs, and barbecued ribs) may be commendable, but the nuggets, made of processed chicken, are deep-fried and may contain nearly 60 per-cent fat.

Perhaps only the wider dissemination of data on the true fat and cholesterol content of the foods we consume can end the self-deception that we are genuinely committed to more healthful, nu-tritious diets. A step in the right direction is the addition of more useful information on food packages due to government and con-sumer pressure in recent years.

On most of the packaged products we now buy in the supermarket is a list of ingredients in order of their abundance in the contents. If sugar heads the list, we are properly warned; if water is listed first in a tomato sauce, we look for another brand. However, the labels do not tell us all we need to know; for example, they do not give percentages. How much beef is in the beef potpie is anyone's guess.

Cholesterol is not generally regarded as a food ingredient. The shopper will often find no cholesterol values listed and must learn to read between the lines, watching for ingredients known to be high in cholesterol: butter, egg yolks, animal fats. (See Appendix, Tables 1 and 2.) Also bear in mind that saturated vegetable fats, principally coconut and palm oils but including hydrogenated (hardened) fats or shortenings, contain no cholesterol but may raise blood cholesterol levels.

Food processors sometimes list cholesterol information, usually when they consider its absence to be a selling point. But the wise shopper is entitled to smile at "No Cholesterol" on the label of a margarine made exclusively from one of the polyunsaturated oils (corn, soybean, cottonseed, or safflower). It is as absurd as if distillers were to put "No Cholesterol" on the labels affixed to bottles of gin.

There is no gainsaying that diet is the primary key to reducing—and controlling—cholesterol. But changing the diet of preference can be a formidable challenge, especially when there is a problem of obesity.

However, when cholesterol is the principal target of attack, a change of diet should be much easier. There are many ways of "getting around" cholesterol, of finding new patterns of eating that keep meals tasting pretty much as they did before—or even better.

We *can* have our (cheese) cake and eat it.

2. Dietary Friends and Enemies

EGGS: NOT SO FRIENDLY

"How do I love thee?" the egg lover might quote Elizabeth Barrett Browning. "Let me count the ways. . . ."

I love thee raw, baked, soft-boiled, hard-boiled, poached, scrambled, sauteed, fried, shirred, deviled, creamed, curried, coddled, glazed, pickled, Benedicted, or Scotched . . . in omelets and soufflés and quiches of infinite variety . . . in mayonnaise and hollandaise and béarnaise . . . in sandwiches and salads and hashes and casseroles . . . in custard and ice cream and in sponge and pound and cheesecakes.

"An egg is always an adventure," said Oscar Wilde.

Or *misadventure*, as the case may be, and probably is.

With the exception of brains and kidneys—hardly staples of most diets—the "incredible edible" egg takes its place at the extreme top end of the cholesterol spectrum. One egg contains as much cholesterol as many people should consume in a whole day, and more than is prudent for some people. It has the cholesterol equivalent of ten hot dogs or a pound and a half of beef.

"As innocent as a new laid egg" goes a simile of librettist W. S. Gilbert. As far as cholesterol is concerned, only the whites of eggs

are innocent; all cholesterol is in the yolks. (Angel food cakes, me-
ringues, and other egg-white confections won't raise dietary cholesterol values. However, excessive sugar may be undesirable for
other reasons.)

The egg yolk does have a relatively high content of polyunsaturated fatty acids but gram for gram raises blood cholesterol more
and faster than any other dietary fat.

There is a great variation, of course, in individual responses to
intakes of dietary cholesterol. When the number of egg yolks eaten
was increased to supply 1000 mg (1 g) of cholesterol a day, some
people showed significantly higher rises in blood cholesterol than
did others. Similarly, when groups of people who habitually consumed at least one egg a day reduced their total dietary cholesterol
intake from 800 mg to 300 mg per day, the decrease in blood cholesterol also ranged widely; the average drop was 3 percent but went
as high as 20 percent. Relatively small increases in dietary cholesterol, depending on the nature of the fat with which they are associated, can in fact bring about highly significant increases in blood
cholesterol. The response in humans seems to be individually determined and may vary with the type of dietary fat consumed.

No one should conclude that the restriction of eggs by itself
will necessarily result in measurable decreases in blood cholesterol.
The Framingham Study, in its earlier phases, did not regulate or in-
quire into the diets of its subjects. These subjects were ordinary
people living and working freely in a normal world. It was reasonable to assume that their egg consumption was not very different
from the population at large; increasing blood cholesterol levels that
were observed could well reflect diets that had considerable cholesterol content from foods other than eggs.

In other volunteers whose diets *were* closely watched, blood
cholesterol levels consistently rose when two whole eggs were eaten
daily. While there is an accompanying increase in bile acid excretion, which carries away some cholesterol, the body is unable to
compensate completely for a chronic dietary cholesterol overload.
As *Nutrition Reviews* observed, the addition of eggs to diets already
fairly high in cholesterol may not appreciably boost blood lipid levels, but the possible effect on hardening the arteries was not readily
determinable. Diets very high in cholesterol (1 g, or 1000 mg, or

more a day) can interfere with the ability of unsaturated vegetable oils to lower blood cholesterol levels, which normally happens when such fats are also present in the diet.

Eggs can be modified before they are laid. The polyunsaturated fatty acid content of the yolk is increased greatly when laying hens are fed a ration containing unsaturated vegetable oils. But the results are not very encouraging. In some experiments, hens maintained normal egg production on diets containing high levels of such unsaturated fats as linseed or safflower oil but the cholesterol content of the eggs changed very little, and feeding such eggs to people didn't help the people at all. However, other research found that egg cholesterol could be reduced as much as 35 percent when hens were given a diet containing sterols, a mixture of compounds derived from plants. But the effect of such eggs on human cholesterol levels has not yet been reported.

The Cleveland Clinic Foundation some years ago sponsored a study involving normal men to compare diets containing ordinary and modified eggs with a diet known to be effective in reducing blood cholesterol. Some men were fed vegetable oils but no eggs, a second group was given two ordinary eggs a day containing an average of 13 percent polyunsaturated fatty acids, and a third group ate two modified eggs a day containing 45 percent polyunsaturated fatty acids. All three diets were similar in total fat but the vegetable oil diet contained only a small fraction of the cholesterol in either the ordinary or modified eggs. The men who ate no eggs at all reduced their cholesterol levels by 19 percent. The men who ate eggs did not, and eggs with increased amounts of polyunsaturated fats showed no advantage over ordinary eggs.

To be fair, it should be pointed out that some respected scientists feel that the "egg threat" has been exaggerated and too shrilly trumpeted. They ask, why proscribe a food that for many is nutritious, palatable, and harmless because a relative few are susceptible to bad effects? While no one is trying to proscribe eggs from the general diet, the fact remains that eggs are extremely high in dietary cholesterol, and many more people have dangerously high blood cholesterol levels than has been previously recognized.

People within the scientific community contend that dietary cholesterol in the range from approximately zero to 600 mg per day may have a decisive effect upon blood cholesterol, but above that range it has little additional effect. In one study, researchers found that feeding an extra egg a day to older men (average age 51) and two extra large eggs to young men (average age 24) caused no significant increase in total blood cholesterol over a period of eight weeks. This result must be interpreted in light of the fact that the usual diets of these men already contained considerable amounts of cholesterol, and eight weeks is a short time in which to effect significant changes in blood cholesterol levels.

Another researcher concluded from a survey of the literature that a consumption of two eggs a day does not normally endanger the cholesterol balance in healthy human adults. This particular conclusion goes contrary to many other studies that establish a relationship between habitual egg-eating and rising blood cholesterol levels, and it assumes that a stable blood cholesterol level precludes the possibility of any atherosclerotic build-up. This study, it should be pointed out, came from the Department of Poultry Science at a large midwestern university.

Methods of preparation of eggs may have a significant influence on their effects. For example, heat, in the presence of oxygen, can induce oxidation. In experiments with animals, eggs prepared in different ways resulted in different blood cholesterol levels. All increased the levels, but the increases were greatest for fried or hard-boiled eggs, considerably less for scrambled or baked eggs, and least for raw or soft-boiled eggs. It is not necessarily so then that an egg is an egg is an egg—the way it is cooked may make a metabolic difference.

For egg lovers who must severely restrict cholesterol consumption, egg substitutes offer one safe compromise. These ersatz eggs are cholesterol-free. A popular type consists of 99 percent egg white and a one-percent mixture of corn oil, gums, emulsifiers, and vitamins. They may not lend themselves to "sunny-side-ups" or poaching but in most other ways are a satisfactory replacement for the real thing. Although they have slightly more sodium than real eggs, they have only about a third the calories, are equal in protein, iron, and calcium, and actually contain more of several vitamins.

Defatted egg powder has comparably desirable virtues. When substituted for whole eggs, it lowers cholesterol blood levels. It also matches regular eggs in nutrient content, minus the dietary fat and cholesterol. Unlike egg substitutes, defatted egg powder is bland and odorless and not very acceptable by itself without some flavoring agent.

It should be noted that room temperature storage of dried, powdered eggs that have not been defatted, or of other foods containing cholesterol, can create sources of possibly harmful derivatives spontaneously formed from the cholesterol. These foods should be stored in well-sealed containers and refrigerated or frozen to prevent oxidation or other forms of chemical deterioration. The egg industry is careful to refrigerate whole eggs quickly after they are laid and delivers them to retail stores within a week where they are again refrigerated.

What is the last word on the egg, then? There is no final word now and perhaps never will be; no warning is likely to apply to everybody.

The best counsel is to be cautious and to go with the facts. The most salient fact is that a single, unadorned large egg provides about 300 mg of dietary cholesterol. For someone restricted to 250 mg daily, that egg is forbidden. Someone limited to 300 mg a day might have an occasional egg on otherwise vegetarian days. Others, particularly men coming into middle age, would do well to keep watch on their blood cholesterol levels; for them it might be wise to start cutting back on eggs and other foods high in cholesterol and saturated fats.

Those who must be especially cholesterol-conscious, because of present condition or family history, should get to know the composition of foods likely to be encountered so that health-promoting choices can be made.

FATS: BENIGN AND OTHERWISE

Total blood cholesterol remains one of the best single predictors of coronary heart disease. Its predictive value is improved if the proportions of low- and high-density lipoproteins are taken into account.

In experiments with daily cholesterol supplements mixed with oil and given to a group of middle-aged men, Ancel Keys and colleagues at the University of Minnesota found relationships between changes in blood cholesterol and additions to dietary cholesterol and between changes in blood cholesterol and dietary supplements of saturated and polyunsaturated fats. Rises in blood cholesterol seemed to be proportional to the square root of the dietary cholesterol supplements. The relation between changes in blood cholesterol and dietary fat supplements can be expressed by the equation

$$\text{Rise in blood cholesterol} = 2.74 \times \text{saturated fat supplement} - 1.31 \times \text{polyunsaturated fat supplement}$$

This says, roughly, that a given increase in dietary saturated fat is about twice as effective in raising blood cholesterol as the same increase in dietary polyunsaturated fat is in lowering it. Thus, if a fat is eaten that is about two parts polyunsaturated and one part saturated, the equation implies that the two components will balance each other, and blood cholesterol should remain unchanged.

Harvard researchers found a somewhat different numerical relationship. In their calculations, rises in blood cholesterol were directly proportional to increases in dietary cholesterol. Eating more cholesterol raises blood cholesterol levels; only the degree seems to be somewhat variable.

Individuals may differ in their body's reactions to dietary fat, but each individual's response is likely to remain relatively constant over time.

Polyunsaturated fatty acids, then, with some reservations, have earned their reputation as the "good" fats. They do help to lower blood cholesterol levels. But that does not mean that more is better;

a pint of corn oil is not preferable to a tablespoon. *Even the best of fats should be consumed in moderation.*

Some fats are needed for health. Our bodies do not manufacture the necessary polyunsaturated fats, so they must be eaten in foods. Necessary fats that must come from diet are called essential fatty acids (EFAs). A deficiency of EFAs can lead to such consequences as irregularities of the heart and circulation and fatty accumulations in the liver. The EFAs also play a role in the synthesis of prostaglandins, a group of important metabolic regulators.

Fatty acids are classified in groups, or families, according to chemical structure (location of the unsatisfied hydrogen atom affinity). EFAs belong to either the omega-3 or omega-6 family. (The omega designation defines the site of the unsaturated double bond within the molecule. The double bond is a force that holds the atoms together in the fatty acid molecule.) For example, the EFA linoleic acid is an omega-6. Its abundant sources are nuts, beans, whole grains, and seed oils. Because this EFA has cholesterol-lowering properties, recommendations have been made to increase the linoleic acid in the diet, advice that has resulted in major dietary shifts in some countries, among them the United States. How the linoleic acid molecule lowers cholesterol is still unclear.

Both omega-6 and omega-3 fatty acids protect against heart disease, but there is still some controversy as to whether omega-3 fatty acids are technically essential. Whether or not they are labeled essential linolenic acid, an omega-3 and a metabolite (breakdown product) of linoleic acid, has been found to lower blood cholesterol about 170 times more than the parent molecule. This suggests that it is the conversion of linoleic acid into linolenic acid that may exert the beneficial effect on blood cholesterol. (Aging, sex, diabetes mellitus, alcohol consumption, catecholamines [a group of substances that can affect the nervous system], trans fatty acids [a type that inhibits the body's ability to use polyunsaturated types], and saturated fats may all have an effect on the enzyme which converts linoleic acid to linolenic acid.) Both healthy volunteers and patients with active heart disease have experienced 17–20 percent reduction in blood cholesterol and 40–67 reductions in triglycerides when omega-3 EFAs from vegetable or fish oils were added to their diets.

The presence of linoleic acid in corn and other vegetable oils probably explains their ability to lower blood cholesterol. Evening primrose oil, an easily absorbed source of both linoleic and linolenic acid, is among the most effective of all the oils; its impact on all but the lowest blood cholesterol levels suggests that it acts physiologically to regulate cholesterol metabolism rather than as a drug. But evening primrose oil is exotic and expensive. Soybean, safflower, and corn oils are also effective and readily available at much lower cost.

How much do alterations in dietary fat accomplish? Even relatively small changes in the polyunsaturated/saturated fatty acid ratio seem to have a general cholesterol-lowering effect. In one study of normal subjects eating about 400 mg of dietary cholesterol daily, LDLs dropped somewhat when only slightly increased amounts of polyunsaturated fats were consumed. The effects were more dramatic when the usual diet contained moderately high to high amounts of cholesterol. The *Journal of Human Nutrition* reported a drop in blood cholesterol of up to 15 percent in a month in a group of normal males, ranging in age from 28 to 46, whose diets were revised to include more polyunsaturated fatty acids and less cholesterol. *Lancet* cited an average 22 percent drop in subjects with high blood cholesterol who were put on severe diets substituting polyunsaturated for saturated fats and supervised for up to 25 months.

Polyunsaturated fats also appear to have a direct effect on high blood pressure (hypertension). A pilot study conducted in Finland, Italy, and the United States revealed more hypertensives among Finns than among either Italians or Americans as well as the consumption of more saturated and less polyunsaturated fats. When the Finnish subjects were placed on a low-fat diet higher in polyunsaturated than saturated fats, blood pressure dropped. An increase of polyunsaturated fats apparently yields double benefits, lower blood pressure and lower blood cholesterol.

However, polyunsaturated fats can be overpraised. There are warnings to be heeded.

The benefits of polyunsaturated oils are more pronounced when the consumption of saturated fats is reduced at the same time. Also, polyunsaturated fats oxidize easily during cooking or storage. Oxidized fats *increase* blood platelet aggregation, clotting, and damage to artery walls.

Some originally polyunsaturated fats are partially hydrogenated (saturated) in being processed into margarine and other products to make them more solid and easier to preserve. Not only do the
"good" fats become more saturated, but hydrogenation converts
much of them from the molecular form called *cis* to the *trans* form
that blocks the body's use of polyunsaturated fat and may also raise
blood cholesterol and harm the arteries.

One interesting study compared two groups of nonsmoking
men of similar age, weight, height, alcohol consumption, and physical activity. The only essential difference was that one group was
vegetarian and had substantially lower blood levels of total cholesterol, LDLs, and triglyceride. The amount of cholesterol eaten by
the vegetarians (with widely varying consumption of eggs) proved
irrelevant. The total intake of fat, however, was another story: Vegetarians whose diet was 35–40 percent fat had appreciably higher
cholesterol and triglyceride levels than vegetarians whose diet was
only 25–33 percent fat.

It has been proposed that, because unsaturated fatty acids take
up more space than saturated fatty acids in the fat molecules into
which they are incorporated, fewer fat molecules can be accommo-
dated by the apoprotein part of LDLs, thus lowering the fat content
of the LDLs.

But even in their purest form, with all their benign actions,
polyunsaturated fats are still fats. Most of us would do well to drastically reduce our total fat consumption while boosting the ratio of
polyunsaturated to saturated fats. All fats are rich in calories, and
calories do count.

FIBER AND OTHER SPECIFIC HELPERS

Food fiber has long been recognized for its ability to dilute calories, to clean teeth, and to soften stools. A reawakened awareness
of its benefits may eventually end the characterization of Western
man as "fat, toothless and constipated." Now there is growing evidence of fiber's potential for lowering cholesterol and enhancing the
health of the heart.

Fiber is an all-inclusive name for a variety of carbohydrates in foods that do not, by themselves, provide nutrients but *do* greatly affect the ways our bodies absorb and use nutrients. The word fiber suggests something in food that has a threadlike texture and needs to be chewed. There is much truth in this, and it can serve as a reminder to eat plenty of plant foods. (Unfortunately, fibers in meat do not count as dietary fiber; a tough steak may need lots of chewing but is not a source of useful fiber.) But the common impression is also a bit misleading. Other plant substances that qualify as dietary fiber may have smooth, thick, gummy, slippery, sticky, or gooey textures.

To the nutritionist, dietary fiber is all the constituents of the cell walls in eaten plant food that are not digested by secretions in the human digestive tract. (Chemical names are pectins, hemicellulose, cellulose, and lignin. See Table 3 in Appendix for pectin content of common foods.)

There are also food substances classified as fiber that are either found naturally as nonstructural parts of plant products or introduced as food additives. (Chemical categories are gums, mucilages, algal polysaccharides, pectins, and chemically modified polysaccharides.)

All fiber components are not equally beneficial. Pectin, for instance, interacts helpfully with LDLs, the major carrier of cholesterol in the body and the principal component of atherosclerotic lesions (plaques) in diseased blood vessels. Cellulose, on the other hand, does *not* seem to be particularly effective in reducing blood cholesterol. When University of Minnesota researchers put a group of middle-aged men on a rigidly controlled diet of natural foods, giving some daily supplements of cellulose and others pectin, cellulose had no discernible effect on blood cholesterol. But within three weeks, the men given pectin averaged a 5-percent reduction. For some reason, water-soluble fibers like pectin and gums reduce cholesterol, while a water-absorbing fiber like cellulose does not. For example, statistically significant retardation of spontaneous atherogenesis was observed in two-year-old cockerels fed a standard diet supplemented with 5 percent pectin for 18 months. (All cockerels eventually developed atherosclerosis, usually between the ages of two to three years.) The pectin-fed birds excreted three times as much fat and almost twice as much cholesterol as did control animals fed the same diet without pectin. The results suggested that pectin may accelerate the passage of food, shorten the time for digestion, and render nutrients less available for absorption. Or it may specifically interfere with the absorption or reabsorption of cholesterol and promote the excretion of cholesterol as such and as bile acids. If pectin does aid in the elimination of bile acids through the intestinal tract, as researchers speculate, it may also forestall the development of gallstones and colon cancer.

Our own discovery of the powers of pectin came about serendipitously during research for the U.S. Army Quartermaster Corps. Dismayed by the fatty deposits autopsies found in the blood vessels of so many of the young casualties of the Korean War, the Army wanted to know if the C rations soldiers ate in the field were a contributing factor inasmuch as they included eggs, meat, and milk powder and were very high in calories.

We experimented with chickens—one of the better animal models for human atherosclerosis—but learned quickly that the chickens rejected the C rations, which were fed to them in a moist, viscous mass they had a hard time eating. Constrained by a limited budget for this research, we purchased some low-cost, dried sugarbeet pulp; adding this to the C-rations made them palatable to the birds. To our surprise, despite the considerable cholesterol and saturated fat in the diet, the chickens' arteries did not collect increased deposits of atherosclerotic plaque. A search of the relevant literature to explain the unexpected results pointed to the possible importance of the pectin in the sugarbeet pulp. This hunch was corroborated by feeding pure pectin to chickens, with good results. Then, in human volunteers, we found that adding pectin to a diet that included two eggs per day prevented the rise in blood cholesterol observed in the control subjects who did not receive pectin.

Common sources of pectin are apples, bananas, citrus fruits, beets, carrots, okra, grapes, berries, and potatoes.

The main function in the body of dietary lignin, another fiber, is to escort bile acids and cholesterol out of the intestines. There is also some evidence that it may prevent the formation of gallstones.

Lignin is present in fair amounts in many foods, including bran and whole-grain cereals, Brazil nuts, peanuts, peaches, pears, strawberries, raspberries, cabbage, tomatoes, peas, Brussels sprouts, spinach, and kale.

Scientists have found various gums—locust bean gum, karaya gum, guar gum, oat gum, and others—particularly effective in lowering blood cholesterol. The explanation is that the sticky gum fibers cling to intestinal bile acids (formed from cholesterol in the liver) and carry them out of the body before they can carry fats back to the liver to feed the cholesterol-creating cycle.

These gums are found in a variety of dried beans, seeds, and other foods such as oatmeal.

No universally accepted methods are yet available for determining the total "useful" fiber content of foods; in fact, data on food fiber is relatively meager. The exception is crude fiber, which may represent only one-fifth to one-half the total fiber in a given food. Crude fiber is defined as the plant material left after digestion first by acid and then by alkali, and can be readily measured.

Measurable or not, fiber is unanimously declared to be "good" for everyone, but, as with other diet components, we are advised to consume it in moderation. Some fiber interacts with other nutrients, such as zinc and other trace minerals, preventing their use by the body. This is particularly true of wheat bran fiber, which contains a phosphorus compound called phytin that strongly binds zinc and iron.

Legumes (vegetables such as peas, beans, and lentils that have pods) and certain other vegetables, fruits, and whole grains have fiber especially effective in lowering blood cholesterol. Among the foods richest in fiber are apples, citrus fruits, bananas, carrots, oats, and all members of the pea-bean family.

To some extent, then, an apple a day does keep the doctor away. Apples and other desirable foods can readily be made part of a healthier daily diet. At breakfast, cholesterol-rich eggs can give way to nutritious, delicious, and easily prepared oatmeal. Chili con carne can be supplanted by a palatable and more healthful meatless chili rich in kidney or pinto beans. Chicken can be rolled in bran, instead of breading made with eggs, for oven baking. A sprinking of grated carrots and chick peas will grace and fortify any green salad. For dessert, fruits in their infinite variety and combinations can gratify an end-of-meal yearning for a taste of something sweet.

Complex carbohydrates, another term frequently used as a synonym for fiber, differ in their effects on cholesterol metabolism. Evidence for the beneficial effects of fiber is accumulating. In a study reported in the *American Journal of Clinical Nutrition* in July 1981, a diet including vegetable leaves, roots, and stalks correlated with lower blood levels of VLDL, LDL, and total cholesterol. A correlation was also found between the eating of whole grains and lower LDL and total cholesterol, but *not* lower VLDL. The findings strongly indicated a health advantage in replacing fat in the diet with vegetable roots, leaves, and stalks and with whole grains. Calorie for calorie, leafy vegetables appeared to be the most effective fiber source in reducing blood cholesterol.

Beans and other legumes have been highly regarded for centuries, but only recently has their ability to combat cholesterol build-up been targeted for study. One of the most impressive research findings comes out of India where it was discovered that the poorest people living around Agra, who subsist largely on chick peas, had much lower cholesterol levels than better-off neighbors who could afford richer, more varied diets. In the Netherlands, Trappist monks were found to have lower blood cholesterol than Benedictine monks; they also depended much more than Benedictines on beans for their staple diet.

Peas, soybeans, lentils, and chick peas have more fiber than most other vegetables. (Baked beans have almost twice as much as broccoli and over twice as much as cabbage.) Their fiber is largely water-soluble, giving legumes their effectiveness as cholesterol-lowering agents. Dr. James W. Anderson, of the University of Kentucky in Lexington, and a colleague found that about four ounces of pinto and navy beans substituted for parts of the usual daily diet of a group of men with very high blood cholesterol brought the levels down by an impressive 19 percent. However, the investigators noted that "While bean-supplemented diets were as effective as oat bran-supplemented diets in lowering serum cholesterol concentrations, oat bran was better tolerated (fewer problems, like intestinal gas) by our patients."

A decade or so ago the Senate Committee on Dietary Goals for the United States—presided over by then Senator George McGovern—recommended increased consumption of starchy foods so that, instead of 22 percent of energy requirements being derived from low-fiber flour, 40–45 percent could better come from high-fiber, whole-grain products. (It also advised reducing the average proportion of dietary fats from 43 to 30 percent of total calories, and sugar from 24 to 15 percent.) Such recommendations, if followed, would be tantamount to going back to a turn-of-the-century diet.

God, according to the Book of Genesis, created plants before fish, animals, and men. "Then take wheat and barley, beans and lentils, millet and spelt," the prophet Ezekiel advised the Jews in Jerusalem. "Mix them together and make your bread out of them."

But there is bread and then there is bread. Much of today's bread is far removed from Ezekiel's "mix."

The Nazis believed that white bread had sapped the fighting will of the German soldiers in World War I and that a switch to rye in World War II would give their troops "the strength and endurance of the Nibelungen." One reason they were happy to sign a pact with the Soviet Union in 1939 was that it gave Germany access, via the Trans-Siberian Railroad, to the protein-rich soybeans it also esteemed.

The war between Japan and China in 1895 and the Russo-Japanese war a decade later were both fought in no small measure for control of the soybeans of Manchuria, sometimes called the Land of the Bean. The Russians were so amazed at the stamina of their opponents, who ate a soy-fortified diet, that as soon as that war ended Russia started an all-out soybean research program. By the time of the Revolution, the soybean was known among the combatants with access to it as "our young Chinese ally."

Dutch scientists studied the diets of three male populations with relatively low blood cholesterol levels: Trappist monks, Arab bedouins, and Yemenite Jews. All these men habitually ate a diet low in total fat and high in complex carbohydrates and vegetable protein. Eating whole-grained bread instead of saturated fats apparently produced low cholesterol levels as effectively as did switching from saturated to polyunsaturated fats in other studies. Whole grains provide the additional benefits of protein, B-complex vitamins, and essential fatty acids.

By and large, cereals, starch roots, and fruits have been the basis of human diet throughout recorded history, the Food and Agriculture Organization of the United Nations has noted, "and this applies to the majority of human beings in the world today." Certain groups of South African blacks, with little choice, adhere to such a diet and have better health as a consequence. They eat foods high in fiber and starch, moderate or low in sugar, and derive protein mostly from vegetable sources. They smoke few cigarettes, drink little alcohol, and are obliged to engage in prolonged daily physical exertion. The cereal fiber is presumed to protect them against such metabolic disorders as constipation, diabetes, and gallstones, as well as atherosclerosis and coronary heart disease. It also quite likely protects against diverticular disease, irritable colon, hemorrhoids, ulcerative colitis, polyps, and cancer of the large bowel.

In a University of Alberta study reported in 1984, fifty subjects with peripheral vascular disease were given either the American Heart Association (AHA) "prudent diet" or a higher-fiber, low-fat diet based on the Pritikin maintenance diet. The caloric intake of the AHA diet group was 49 percent carbohydrate, 20 percent protein, and 31 percent fat; percentages for the other group were 64, 22, and 14, respectively. The AHA diet averaged 201 mg cholesterol and 23 g (grams) fiber per day; the other group received 108 mg cholesterol and 43 g fiber. All were encouraged to exercise regularly, consume less salt, caffeine, and alcohol, and restrict cigarette smoking as much as possible. Diet counseling was provided, and subjects were kept under examination for a year.

Both groups decreased blood levels of triglycerides, LDL, and total cholesterol, and increased HDL levels, but the drop in cholesterol was especially significant in the high-fiber group. The researchers concluded that both dietary regimens, combined with exercise, can be very beneficial to patients with peripheral vascular disease (poor circulation in arms and legs). The correlation between high dietary fiber and low blood cholesterol seems quite consistent.

There is also a correlation between the consumption of fiber and a reduced incidence of colorectal cancer. This cancer-protective effect stems from the capacity of various fibers to bind cholesterol and related compounds in the large intestine. Researchers at the U.S. Citrus and Subtropical Products Laboratory have ranked various fruits and vegetables according to their ability to bind cholesterol. Sweet potatoes score highest at 30 percent. Cellulose has a binding capacity of 20 percent, and lignin, 16 percent. Citrus pectin at 8 percent is a relatively poor binder. No natural food came near the 84 percent of the cholesterol-lowering drug cholestyramine. But the natural foods taste infinitely better, provide nourishment, cost less, and have few side effects.

How much fiber should we include in our diet? Some Africans consume as much as 150 g a day and are relatively free of degenerative diseases. The average intake in Europe and North America is 25 g or less a day. Most experts agree that this is too little; many suggest a minimum of 30 g, but increases should be undertaken gradually to give the body time to adjust.

Since the time of Hippocrates, it has been observed that wheat bran is a laxative. Arab physicians of the Middle Ages and Shakespeare's Coriolanus praised the satisfying and laxative qualities of dark bread while castigating white bread. A common saying among the Puritans was, "Brown bread and the Gospel are good fare."

As early as 1923 the cereal manufacturer Will Keith Kellogg advocated the use of wheat bran. Before that, Sylvester Graham introduced graham crackers to the world. Adding wheat bran to our diet has many benefits. It will alleviate constipation, ease hemmorrhoids, relieve diverticulitis, and help in some cases of irritable bowel syndrome. It may also improve carbohydrate (sugar) tolerance slightly, English scientists have observed. But it will not cure diabetes, reduce excessive fatty substances in the blood (hyperlipidemia), or reverse hardening of the arteries. However, large amounts of whole cereal are far more beneficial than simply adding bran to white flour.

Oat bran, however, is another story. It measurably reduces blood cholesterol in men with high levels. It is rich in water-soluble fiber and brings down LDLs. It is palatable as hot cereal and can be incorporated into muffins, breads, cookies, meat loaf, and other foods.

"LDL cholesterol can be reduced up to 20 percent in people with high levels just by consuming a cup of oat bran a day," declares Dr. Jon Story of Purdue University. However, he warns that adding oat bran to the diet is not a license to continue bad eating habits.

The blood cholesterol-lowering effect of whole ground oats and its components was also studied in chicks fed high-cholesterol diets. Oat hulls were very effective, but oat starch and oat oil had no such beneficial action. Liver fats and cholesterol were significantly reduced by whole oats and oat hulls, and to a lesser extent, by dehulled oats.

"If something smells so bad, it surely must be good for you." Well, not necessarily, in view of the noxious odors that assail us on this increasingly polluted planet. But for garlic, the axiom is unarguably true. Garlic's credentials are formidable and rooted in history.

The Codex Ebers, an Egyptian medical papyrus written about 3500 years ago, suggested twenty-two garlic-based remedies for malaises ranging from sensations of weakness, to headaches, to tumor of the throat. Pliny the Elder, the Roman encyclopedist, went the Codex one better with no fewer than sixty-one "complaints" (hoarseness, hemorrhoids, epilepsy, and tuberculosis among them) for which garlic was the recommended palliative. Hippocrates himself used the bulbous herb as a laxative and diuretic. Aristotle endorsed it as a cure for rabies, Mohammed for the treatment of scorpion stings, and the great Greek physician Galen as a "heal-all."

In countries where garlic is consumed regularly and copiously, the health benefits are conspicuous and documentable. The incidence of heart disease is very low. Garlic demonstrably lowers total cholesterol levels, and is associated with higher HDL and lower LDL levels. It is also thought by many to protect against strokes, cancer, and diabetes, as well as to possess antibiotic-like properties.

Under the supervision of Tagore Medical College in India, sixty-two heart patients were divided into two groups, one fed garlic daily. Over a period of eight months, the garlic eaters had significant decreases in triglycerides, cholesterol, and risk of heart attack, in contrast to the control group whose cholesterol levels did not change.

Other researchers have found that garlic oil can inhibit clot formation, a deterrent in itself to heart attacks and strokes. It is this oil fraction that is the active anti-plaque constituent. Garlic oil has repeatedly been shown to have cholesterol-lowering activity in both healthy people and cardiac patients.

Onions are closely allied to garlic in biological effects. A substance has been isolated from onions that also keeps blood platelets from sticking together; the clumping of these cells is a crucial step in the formation of blood clots. Onions, too, have an oil that is effective in stimulating fibrinolytic activity (breaking down of a fibrous protein present in the clotting of blood).

The essential oils of garlic and onion are chemically a combination of sulfur-containing compounds (mainly allyl propyl disulphide and diallyl disulphide). Consumption of the essential oil fraction alone, which contains all the taste and odor, exactly duplicates the beneficial effects of eating the whole garlic or onion (raw or cooked). Research reported in the journal *Atherosclerosis* established the protective action of garlic and onions against fat-induced increases in blood cholesterol and credits them with decreases in blood coagulation time.

Fragile-appearing alfalfa sprouts also have special strengths. My colleague Paul Griminger and I found a decrease in blood cholesterol (and in liver cholesterol) among chicks fed cholesterol and saponins (a plant substance that produces a soapy lather) simultaneously. Saponins, which form stable complexes with cholesterol, occur in alfalfa sprouts.

If you poll authorities on diet and nutrition for a list of a dozen "super-foods," the chances are strong that mushrooms will usually be cited, along with citrus fruits, milk, oatmeal, apples, and spinach.

Within the last two decades, mushrooms have won special regard for their cholesterol-lowering powers. Much of the research has come out of Japan, where, in recent years, half the deaths of middle-aged or older people have been attributed to either myocardial infarction (traceable to hardening of the arteries) or encephalomalacia (softening of the brain caused by the degeneration of brain blood vessels.)

The shiitake, or Japanese forest mushroom, so popular now in the United States, was repeatedly tested by addition to sukiyaki, pork stew, and other Japanese staple dishes with a high saturated fat content. The food tasted even better and provided the even greater blessing of lowering blood cholesterol levels.

Eritadenine, a derivative isolated from the Japanese mushroom *Lentinus edoes*, was tested in animals and not only lowered all blood lipid levels but was more than *ten times* as effective as the drug clofibrate. As reported in *Atherosclerosis*, its benefits also came swiftly, within three hours.

Avocados, those highly edible, buttery fruits, are often denigrated as fatty and fattening. They do contain 20 percent fat, but 85 percent of this fat is unsaturated. In an avocado-feeding test in Florida with a group of men ranging in age from 27 to 72, more than half of the men lost body weight, and their blood cholesterol levels decreased significantly, between 9 and 43 percent.

PLANT STEROLS: THE ABSORBERS

Cholesterol absorption, simply stated, is the extent to which dietary cholesterol is absorbed before becoming cholesterol in the bloodstream. Obviously there is a direct relationship between the kinds of food we eat and our blood lipid levels, but it is not one-to-one. A daily consumption of 600–700 mg of dietary cholesterol does not produce a 600–700 mg blood cholesterol level.

Nor can the dietary-bloodstream cholesterol relationship be expressed by a formula applicable to everybody. Many people can eat foods reasonably high in cholesterol without developing a "cholesterol problem"; others must be tirelessly vigilant about what they eat to keep their cholesterol levels from soaring. Heredity and constitutional differences, not cholesterol intake by itself, are the governing factors.

Cholesterol is absorbed exclusively in the small intestine, and preferentially in the half farther from the stomach. By using radioactively labeled cholesterol, scientists have determined that there is a delay of 24 to 72 hours before cholesterol in food consumed is reflected in peak cholesterol levels in the bloodstream.

The average maximum intestinal capacity of subjects to absorb cholesterol, according to research summarized in the *Journal of Applied Physiology*, is 2 g (2000 mg) per day, about twice the estimated daily synthesis of cholesterol in the liver.

Cholesterol is absorbed in three stages: the dispersion of cholesterol in micellar form (small particles); passage into and through the mucosal cells that line the inside of the intestine; and combination with other fats into chylomicrons, which enter the lymph circulation. Plant substances called sterols are known to inhibit cholesterol absorption, perhaps by interfering in the exchange process necessary for the transport of cholesterol through the mucous lining.

Plant sterols such as beta-sitosterol and campesterol are fatty alcohols found in a wide variety of vegetables, grains, and seeds, including eggplant, cabbage, soybeans, peanuts, rice, yams, barley, and avocados; particularly rich sources are soybean and corn oils.

Cholesterol absorption decreases when plant sterols are added to dietary fat. In tests, when dietary fat was 1 percent cholesterol, the addition of 2 percent plant sterols resulted in a 30-percent reduction in cholesterol absorption. A greater increase in the amount of plant sterols in the diet produced an even larger decrease in cholesterol absorption.

The influence of absorbed dietary cholesterol on blood cholesterol was studied in Seventh Day Adventists, who are vegetarians, and compared with nonvegetarian groups. The Seventh Day Adventists had significantly lower levels of blood cholesterol and triglycerides. Both their dietary intake and *percentage* absorption of cholesterol were also lower.

In another study, university students (73 men and 19 women) on a special ration, 45 percent of whose calories were in butter fat, were given supplements of a commercial preparation of the sterol beta-sitosterol ranging from 50 to over 6000 mg (6 g). Starting with the 300-mg supplements, sitosterol increments caused progressively larger decreases in blood cholesterol levels.

In still another study, reported in the *Canadian Journal of Biochemistry and Physiology*, young men received 60 percent of their calories as butterfat, and sitosterol supplements again significantly reduced blood cholesterol. Blood cholesterol also appreciably decreased when the total dietary fat was divided calorically into equal parts of butterfat and sitosterol-rich corn oil.

There is evidence that sterols from the sea—from brown algae such as kelp, a staple of the diet of Japanese and other cultures highly dependent on seafood—can also diminish blood cholesterol levels.

FISH AND FISH OILS

Just when the message was getting through that many of us would do well to avoid fatty fish and shellfish (because of their fat and cholesterol content, respectively), we now learn that these fish contain polyunsaturated fatty acids that can lower cholesterol and inhibit the tendency of blood cells to form artery-blocking clots. Large amounts of two such fatty acids—eicosapentaenoic (EPA) and docosahexaenoic (DHA)—may be even more beneficial than polyunsaturated vegetable oils in reducing the risk of heart attack. They may also be essential for certain organ systems, especially the brain, to develop properly.

Collectively, these protective substances—known as omega-3 long-chain fatty acids—have lowered cholesterol and triglyceride blood levels and reduced both the quantity and adhesiveness of clot-forming blood platelets when consumed in the equivalent of five servings of fish a week. They may also reduce the formation of fatty plaques. Researchers writing in the *British Journal of Nutrition* have hypothesized that populations that live largely on fish or marine mammals may be less prone to coronary heart disease because of their higher intake of EPA and DHA.

Eskimos living in Point Hope, Alaska, represent one of the few remnants of whale-, seal-, and walrus-hunting cultures left in the world. In summer they capture from three to seven 4-ton whales; the meat and fat are distributed and preserved. Seal, walrus, small amounts of fish, and some caribou are also caught during these brief summers. The long dark winters often bring famines, sometimes relieved by the occasional capture of a polar bear. Cholesterol is quite low in the meats of sea mammals but can be three times as high (e.g., in seals) in the fat.

The Eskimos studied ate 520–1650 mg of cholesterol daily. Their average total blood cholesterol was 221 mg but there were only four instances of heart disease per thousand, compared with more than ten times that number in the American population at the time of the study. However, it should be pointed out that the Eskimos were relatively young—half under 26—and coronary heart disease does not usually manifest itself until the forties or fifties. Still, levels of blood cholesterol rarely exceeded 250 mg, and these occurred only in the three percent of the Eskimos who were over 40 years old.

Commenting on the high levels of EPA intake among the Eskimos of northwestern Greenland and their low incidence of heart disease, an observer reported in *Lancet* that delayed atherosclerosis might be attributed to the low concentration of total cholesterol, LDLs, and VLDLs and the high HDL levels in male Eskimos. *Nutrition Reviews* has pointed out that Greenland Eskimos have lower blood cholesterol and lipoprotein levels and much lower triglycerides than do mainland Danes, and makes this dietary distinction: marine oils high in EPA offer even more protection than do the polyunsaturated vegetable oils now popular in Denmark and other Western countries.

Eating fish (or fish oils) may offer protection against coronary heart disease, a twenty-year mortality study from Holland and a short-term investigation from Oregon both suggest. In the Dutch study, the twenty-year mortality rate from heart disease was more than 50 percent lower among those who consumed about one ounce of fish per day compared with nonfish eaters. In the Oregon study, patients with high blood lipid levels showed sharp decreases in blood cholesterol (27 percent) and triglyceride (64 percent) levels on a fish oil diet compared with either a low-fat controlled diet or a vegetable oil diet rich in linoleic acid. The authors of both studies concluded that fish (or fish oils) may be of great benefit in the prevention of coronary heart disease as well as in the treatment of high blood lipid levels.

Among the "fatty" fishes coming back into favor are mackerel, salmon, bluefish, sardines, mullet, rainbow trout, lake trout, herring, tuna, sablefish, shad, butterfish, and pompano. Shellfish are quite low in fat, but the fat they do contain is relatively high in the valuable omega-3 fatty acids EPA and DHA.

Most shellfish do not have as much cholesterol as once thought. Clams, mussels, oysters, and scallops are very low in cholesterol. Lobster, shrimp, and crabs have considerably more, but not much more than meat and poultry, and their low fat content makes them desirable foods for people who must watch their weight as well as their hearts. Even when dietary cholesterol is severely restricted, shrimp may be enjoyed on occasion.

A few general advisories on fish and fish oils may be useful.

Fish oils are available in the form of supplements, but why not spend less and enjoy fish as the entree of a good balanced meal.

Neither fish nor fish oils, however frequently consumed, will give anyone a safe license to indulge in eggs, meat, butterfat, and hard cheese.

Prize canned fish for itself, not for any oils it may be packed in. In fact, it's better to choose canned fish packed in water or tomato sauce. But tomato sauce can be very salty, so brands labeled low-sodium or no-salt-added are preferable. Canned tuna is now available with 50–60 percent less salt than before.

Fresh fish is naturally low in sodium, even saltwater fish, its salty environment notwithstanding.

For cholesterol-cautious shoppers, the fish most to be avoided are those breaded and fried (they often contain more bread and fat than fish) and those swimming in fatty sauces. The best way to prepare fish is to broil, bake, poach, steam, or pan-fry in very little oil. Broiling fish retains nearly all its natural nutrients; frying causes the greatest nutritional losses.

Ocean fish generally present less of a pollution problem than fresh-water fish. However, the larger predators—notably tuna and swordfish—tend to accumulate chemical pollutants. Fresh-water fish from lakes or streams may contain infectious parasites.

Writing in the *New York Times*, health and nutrition columnist Jane E. Brody has extolled fish as an excellent source of essential nutrients. Canned sardines, salmon, and mackerel (eaten bones and all) are rich in calcium, the bone-building nutrient deficient in too many American diets. Hard-shelled clams and oysters have considerable iron and a three-and-one-half ounce can of sardines or tuna furnishes 40 percent of the daily protein requirement of adults.

Mackerel and herring were compared for specific cardiovascular benefits in a study described in *Atherosclerosis* in 1983. After a period of eating mackerel on a daily basis, the subjects showed a marked decline in total cholesterol, tryglycerides, and lecithin cholesterol acyl transferase (LCAT, an enzyme involved with cholesterol metabolism and its eventual excretion) activity. But after the herring-eating period, changes in blood lipids were minor, except for a decrease in LCAT activity. Because mackerel also lowered blood pressure, it obviously offers cardiovascular benefits.

Cod liver oil is also rich in omega-3 fatty acids. A group of volunteers in an experiment conducted in Germany ended up with lower blood pressure and cholesterol. But taking large amounts of cod liver oil poses the threat of toxic doses of vitamins A and D.

Fish is generally good for you, but a warning bears repeating. "You simply can't take fish oil and go on eating all the eggs, bacon, meat and butterfat you want," cautioned Dr. William E. Connor, a leading researcher in cholesterol and heart disease at Oregon Health Science University in Portland.

SPECIFIC NUTRIENTS AND WATER

Other dietary substances may be relevant to the health of our hearts, among them vitamins C and E, chromium, calcium, and water (including hardness or softness).

Although many claims are made for the health-giving powers of vitamin C, there is no conclusive evidence at present that it has any cholesterol-lowering effect. The results of several studies disagree with one another.

Vitamin E, administered in amounts of 50 to 90 International Units daily, has been reported to reduce levels of cholesterol (up to 35 percent) and triglycerides. This vitamin is a good antioxidant and as such it protects essential fatty acids in our bodies; it may also protect our arteries against the type of oxidative damage that can bring on heart disease. Vitamin E is present in most vegetable oils, and wheat germ oil, whole wheat, and wheat germ are especially good sources.

Supplements of calcium carbonate, according to research summarized in *Lipids*, may have long-term value in reducing plaque formation and delaying the onset of atherosclerotic heart disease. A group of eight men and two women with high blood cholesterol were given 2 g of supplemental dietary calcium carbonate daily for a year, resulting in a decrease of 25 percent in blood cholesterol and a significant decrease in triglycerides.

In a study reported in the *American Journal of Clinical Nutrition*, students whose diets contained varying amounts of different fats were given two different levels of calcium supplements. A small amount of calcium added to a diet high in saturated fats did not stop a rise in blood cholesterol levels. Small and large amounts had no effect on total blood cholesterol in the students whose diets were relatively high in polyunsaturated fats. But the addition of 2 g of calcium to highly saturated-fat diets measurably lowered the amount of cholesterol in the bloodstream.

Water also seems to influence the health of the heart. The softer the drinking water, the higher the cardiovascular death rate, according to the London School of Hygiene and Tropical Medicine on the basis of an epidemiological study in Japan, the United States, the United Kingdom, Sweden, and Ireland, performed some years ago.

Researchers concluded that the minerals in hard water—calcium, vanadium, magnesium, chromium, and lithium—presumably have a good influence on lipid metabolism. Other evidence for the effect of water appeared in the *Journal of the American Medical Association*. A state-by-state analysis, covering 163 municipalities, of the deaths of middle-aged men from heart-related disease showed a clear correlation between hardness of water and lower total death rates, as well as lower mortality from coronary heart disease and other cardiovascular diseases. In general, Atlantic seaboard states had softer water and higher death rates for men in the 45–64 age bracket; New Mexico had the lowest death rate—290.2 per 100,000 population—and South Carolina the highest—511.4 per 100,000.

It is possible that calcium in hard water is an important adjunct to calcium in our food and probably helps inhibit the absorption of such toxic elements as lead, cadmium, and cobalt that come from the soil and water pipes. Calcium can also combine in the digestive tract with saturated fatty acids and, through soap formation, prevent their absorption into the bloodstream.

In most drinking water the concentration of sodium is low, but artificial softening can boost the sodium content because a common method of softening water exchanges sodium for calcium. This increase in sodium is counterindicated for many people with high blood pressure and other disorders.

The difference between hard and soft drinking water can amount to 200 mg of calcium per day. It has been estimated that less than 30 percent of the calcium we ingest is absorbed, so the importance of drinking hard water as a source of calcium may be greater than usually realized.

SUGAR

The average American consumes 120 pounds of sugar and other caloric sweeteners a year. That comes to a startling 600 calories of sweetening a day! It may seem unlikely at first, but a look at the sweeteners in many of our favorite ready-made foods provides clear evidence.

It does not matter much, from the body's point of view, whether sweeteners are refined sugars (sucrose)—like white table sugar, brown sugar, and confectioners sugar—raw sugar, or honey. Fructose, the sugar found in fruits and corn syrup (used in many processed foods), is metabolized more slowly than sucrose and without a large release of insulin, which makes it preferable for diabetics. Only blackstrap molasses carries enough essential nutrients, calcium and potassium, to justify a claim of being more than empty calories.

Sugar was once placed alongside saturated fat and cholesterol as a major risk factor in coronary heart disease. However, many clinical observations, animal experiments, and epidemiological studies later, it appears not to be so. The trouble with sugar lies elsewhere.

All carbohydrates are not the same. Sugar and starch are both carbohydrates, one refined, the other complex. A body of research has established that cholesterol drops if sugar in the diet is replaced with leafy vegetables, whole grains, and the carbohydrates from legumes (peas, beans). Interestingly, though, the decrease does not always occur when sugar is replaced with the carbohydrates from bread or potatoes.

Scientists Robert E. Hodges and W. H. Krehl, writing in *The American Journal of Clinical Nutrition*, observed during a short-term study that subjects complained of hunger on a diet high in sucrose but often felt "stuffed" on sugar-free diets containing complex carbohydrates. The diet high in refined sugars and carbohydrates raised blood cholesterol and other lipids, while the diet high in complex carbohydrates lowered them.

Even if too much sugar in foods and drinks presents no direct health problem, it displaces our appetite for more nourishing, health-enhancing nutrients our bodies need. Empty calories from sugar usurp the place of complex carbohydrates, protein, vitamins, and minerals. But a sensible diet will not cut out sweets entirely. Small amounts of sugar and other sweeteners heighten flavors, provide quick energy, raise our spirits, and add pleasure to life.

MILK, COFFEE, AND ALCOHOL

Generations were taught from childhood that milk is "the perfect food." A quart of milk a day, along with the apple, would keep the doctor away. For youngsters, milk was the *sine qua non* for growth and the development of sturdy bones and strong teeth. Especially rich in protein and calcium, it also had some of nearly all the other essential nutrients. "The object of this war [the Second World War]," declared Vice President Henry A. Wallace in 1942, "is to make sure that everybody in the world has the privilege of drinking a quart of milk a day."

Today, even with the spread of famine, Mr. Wallace would not regard a quart of milk a day as the "privilege" of everybody in the world. Custom, cultural taboos, and differences in the human constitution make milk an unsatisfactory food for many peoples. Mother's milk—taken at the breast—will always be an unassailable blessing for the newborn child, but we are now aware that many members of some groups, such as blacks, Asians, and some Mediterranean populations, cannot tolerate cow's milk at all. Many Caucasian children are allergic to it, and many adults have a lowered tolerance for it.

We have been cautioned about the high fat content of whole milk and told to drink skim milk because it is almost devoid of fat and provides only half the calories of whole milk. But the full story is more complicated than this.

Milk apparently contains a cholesterol-lowering factor, which has not yet been identified and which pasteurization may destroy. There is evidence, paradoxically, that this factor tends to keep blood cholesterol from rising whether one consumes fatty whole milk or fat-free skim milk, but consumption of concentrated butterfat equivalent to the dietary fat and cholesterol in whole milk results in an increase of blood cholesterol. Also, some nomadic, cattle-herding tribes of East Africa (as noted earlier) subsist almost entirely on milk and occasional small amounts of meat yet do not develop atherosclerosis. Their habitually vigorous physical exertion may be a partial explanation. Nevertheless, when a group of Masai men were given excessive amounts of whole milk in an experiment, all gained weight rapidly, a frequent precursor to rising blood cholesterol, but their cholesterol levels actually declined.

There is some evidence that in children and young adults, the rate of liver synthesis of cholesterol falls in response to some components in cow's milk, but this response apparently declines with age. Skim milk, in a test with adolescent boys, appeared to have a cholesterol-lowering effect, but this may be partly attributable to its low cholesterol and fat content. Other research has found yogurt to be cholesterol-lowering even when made from whole milk.

One study gave different groups of healthy young volunteers sizeable daily supplements, respectively, of whole milk, skim milk, yogurt, buttermilk, or sweet acidophilus milk (for those sensitive to lactose) for a three-week period. The added calories produced a general increase in weight, especially in those given yogurt or acidophilus milk, but no measurable increases in blood cholesterol. The results suggested that the regular consumption of large amounts of milk products by young adults, at least for short periods, is not likely to cause major changes in blood lipids.

Yogurt and calcium supplements were used in separate tests with young men and women at the University of North Carolina, Greensboro. The women's total blood cholesterol rose substantially with yogurt supplements and to a lesser extent with calcium, but the men's did not change appreciably. One speculation was that men absorb calcium more efficiently than do females.

Whatever it is in milk and yogurt that may lower blood cholesterol, calcium is probably a factor.

Coffee, unlike milk, is not cherished for its nutritive benefits. There are many reasons to limit the amount of coffee we drink, and one of them has to do with cholesterol. A study from Norway, reported in *The New England Journal of Medicine*, implies that the more coffee drunk, the higher the cholesterol levels. Nearly 15,000 men and women drank from less than one to more than nine cups of coffee a day. Consumption exceeding nine cups a day increased the blood cholesterol levels by an average of 30 mg, 14 percent above the levels of those who drank one cup or less a day. HDLs were not much changed, which means that the increases were of LDLs, the contributors to build-ups of fatty deposits in the arteries.

Cream and sugar might be suspect, but since 80 percent of the Norwegians in the study drank their coffee black, caffeine is the likely offender. If caffeine is at fault, then tea and cola drinks would be expected to produce similar responses.

Researchers at Stanford have confirmed the European studies pointing to a relationship between coffee drinking and cholesterol. Their findings, released in the winter of 1985, established the "risk threshold" at two and one-quarter cups a day. Earlier, the Boston Collaborative Drug Surveillance Program, conducted at Boston University Medical Center, found a positive association between coffee consumption and acute myocardial infarction. If caffeine, also present in tea, is the contributing factor, it is curious that neither the Stanford nor the Boston study detected a risk for tea drinking.

If cholesterol were the only consideration, people with low cholesterol levels could drink coffee freely, while others with higher levels should prudently cut down or switch to decaffeinated beverages. However, caffeine is an adrenaline-stimulating drug that increases heart irregularities and the risk of possibly fatal cardiac arrests. It also reduces the effectiveness of medication used to treat angina heart pain and high blood pressure.

Alcohol as a beverage introduces considerations very different from those of milk and coffee. "A jug of wine, a loaf of bread—and thou. . . ." paints a pretty picture, and a loaf of bread (particularly one made from whole grains) and thou are indisputable blessings. But the jug of wine may be something else.

There is much to be said—and it frequently *is* said—for the consumption of alcoholic beverages in moderation. For example, the prestigious *Harvard Medical School Health Letter* has averred that people are better off drinking up to three ounces of distilled spirits (or the equivalent in wine or beer) than drinking nothing at all. Some studies even indicate that the more drinking, even to excess, the less atherosclerosis, but other studies do not confirm, and some even contradict this.

It is possible that, because alcohol relaxes the central nervous system, it may sometimes be a boon, especially to individuals under stress. Small amounts may also have a soothing effect on some blood vessels. It may also be that alcohol stops red blood cells from forming clots that can clog arteries. A study conducted at King's College in London suggested that wine taken with a rich meal can help prevent blood clumping. The rate of blood clumping in volunteers was checked under three different conditions: (1) after they drank five 5-ounce glasses of white wine, (2) after they ate a meal (without wine) high in saturated fats, and (3) after they drank the wine with their meal. Wine alone did not inhibit blood clumping;

the fatty meal by itself increased blood clumping; when the wine was drunk with the meal, much less clumping occurred.

Alcohol has been shown to raise blood HDL levels. However, scientists have recently separated HDL into subgroups and found that not all are necessarily protective. HDL_2, the subgroup raised by exercise, apparently is, but HDL_3 apparently is not. It is not clear which HDL alcohol raises.

There are obvious cautions about alcohol. Some people are allergic to it. Drinking and driving can be fatal. Like other drugs, it is potentially addictive. Its calories are high and empty. Small amounts of alcohol stimulate appetite and invite the danger of overeating and putting on unwanted pounds. While drinking may confer one healthful benefit, it may simultaneously contribute to health threats.

Whether to go on—or to start—drinking in moderation for the sake of heart health is best answered by a personal physician who knows an individual's medical history.

3. Exercise: The Second Best Regulator

N ext to dietary reform, regular exercise is perhaps the surest way to "fight cholesterol."

A definite relationship has been found between exercise and blood cholesterol levels.

Considerable research, here and abroad, affirms that continuing physical activity helps to reduce the risk of coronary heart disease.

Exercise seems to have an important impact on increasing the ratio of the desirable HDLs to total cholesterol, though not all studies are in agreement. How is a matter of speculation. Perhaps it tends to eliminate VLDLs and LDLs by using triglycerides as fuel for working muscles, thus starving the lipoproteins for fat supplies.

"When I feel the urge to exercise," the late Robert Maynard Hutchins, President of the University of Chicago once declared, "I lie down until it passes."

"I have never taken any exercise," confessed Mark Twain, "except for sleeping and resting. And I never intend to try any. Exercise is loathsome."

Even today many people concur with these sentiments, but fewer can defend them as the better part of wisdom. More are like James Michener, the perennially best-selling novelist, who survived a "stupendous" heart attack two decades ago. He credits regular exercise as a key component of his sustained well-being. Describing his ordeal in "An Ailing Heart," which appeared in the *New York Times Sunday Magazine*, Mr. Michener quoted his attending physician, the late Dr. Paul Dudley White: "A sedentary life carries risks. Now obviously, many men lead perfectly happy lives without ever moving from their easy chairs. But I notice that those who boast, 'The only exercise I ever take is serving as pallbearer at the burial of my tennis playing friends,' are the ones who die in their early 60s. And a prolonged sedentary life followed by a resumption of vigorous exercise is most unwise." Dr. White himself practiced what he preached. He ate a low-cholesterol diet, bicycled regularly, and lived to 87.

The important Framingham Study neglected to emphasize or accurately assess the physical activity of its subjects. The theory was that the general level of activity could be inferred from three items on which there were available data: weight gain, vital capacity of the lungs, and resting pulse rates. But these are, to say the least, not very comprehensive indicators.

Comparisons of occupations can illuminate the varying amounts of physical activity certain groups perform and may point to corresponding risks for heart disease, but not necessarily or conclusively. In one such comparison, in communal settlements in Israel, men whose job required hard physical exertion had a lower incidence of coronary heart disease than men who performed sedentary tasks. Diet could not be a factor because everyone ate in a common dining room and all were offered the same food—single portions of meat and "rich" foods (probably pastry-type desserts) supplemented with bread, potatoes, and the like as energy needs demanded. The diet of the more active men, true, derived a smaller proportion of its calories from the meat and "rich" food than did the diet of the sedentary men.

Also, in London, postal clerks were found to have higher coronary heart disease rates than postmen who deliver the mail. (This finding coincides with a report on District of Columbia postal workers.) London bus drivers were more prone to die of coronary heart disease than the more active conductors who go up and down the steps of the double-deckers collecting fares. The drivers were also heavier, had much higher blood cholesterol levels, and were twice as likely to have high blood pressure. Interestingly, the postal employees and busmen were more inclined to change from more to less active jobs (mail deliverers to clerks and conductors to drivers) than in the other direction when the opportunity arose, though the pay was approximately the same.

However, a study of a Swiss Alpine population found low blood cholesterol despite an intake high in calories and saturated fat. Much of their diet derived from cheese, whole milk, cream, butter, and meat. Factors of weight, fatty tissue, altitude, climate, and smoking habits did not differentiate them from other groups studied. On the other hand, the population of the Swiss city Basel had blood cholesterol levels comparable to those of the United States. What set the Alpine villagers apart, it was concluded, was exercise. The villagers were constantly involved in intense physical activity because their agricultural work forced them to walk long distances and up and down hills. The Basel city dwellers were much less active, even though only 10 percent of the families owned cars at the time of the study. It was speculated that saturated fat may be less important than physical activity, or that its effect becomes more apparent when a population is physically inactive.

An occupational analysis was also made of 228 Caucasian men in the New York City area who died suddenly under the age of 55 of coronary heart disease confirmed by autopsy. The occupations had been sedentary for 49 percent, moderately active for 35 percent, and strenuous for only 16 percent. The conclusion was that heavy physical activity protected against sudden death from coronary heart disease, but not to the exclusion of other factors.

It was recently observed that symphony conductors seemed to enjoy extraordinarily long lives. The roster of luminaries who were still active in their eighties and beyond is impressive: Leopold Stokowski, Arturo Toscanini, Otto Klemperer, Pierre Monteux, Arthur Fiedler, Sir Adrian Bolt, Eugene Ormandy, Bruno Walter. These maestros obviously loved their work and did not have to face obligatory retirement at 65 or 70. But they were also on their feet nearly all their working day, and their arms and torsos were almost constantly in vigorous motion.

But occupation alone is not a reliable gauge of the amount of

energy a person expends, not in an age that no longer heeds the bib-
lical injunction, "By the sweat of thy brow shalt thou eat bread."

A case in point is the 1974 monograph *Coronary Heart Disease—The Global Picture* by Ancel Keys, in which he reported the
results of a study of some 16,000 male British civil servants between the ages of 40 and 64. Comparisons were made between those
who stayed well and those who developed coronary heart disease.
A significantly higher percentage of the healthy men engaged in
leisure-time vigorous exercise, in contrast to the men who became
coronary victims. Those who exercised only lightly or irregularly
had about the same propensity for developing heart disease.

So there is now less of a connection between job and total physical activity because of expanding leisure time and health-conscious-
ness and the proliferation of health spas, tennis courts, bicycle
lanes, jogging tracks, hiking clubs, "fitness" vacations, and mara-
thon races. Office buildings, apartment houses, hotels, motels, cities, and villages are all providing new facilities to encourage people
to exercise.

In another British study reported in the *British Medical Journal*, 15,171 men between the ages of 25 and 74 showed a significant
association between physical activity, at both work and leisure, and
lower blood cholesterol levels and blood pressure. In men under 60,
nonactive leisure also correlated with relatively heavier weight and
cigarette smoking. Thus, although strenuous leisure activity reduced the risk of coronary heart disease in young and middle-aged
men, benefits were not necessarily all due to exercise. During their
leisure hours these men may also have smoked less and eaten more
prudently for personal, psychological, or cultural reasons.

The likely link between lack of exercise and coronary heart
disease perhaps explains why people in less-developed countries
generally seem to have less heart disease, and why, in many countries—probably including the United States—heart attacks are less
common in rural than in urban populations. The records of local physicians in North Dakota, for example, indicate that coronary heart
disease is rarer among farmers than among town or city dwellers.

Comparisons between geographically separated brothers can

be revealing. Almost 2000 brothers, all Irish-born, were selected for a study to compare those who had remained in Ireland with those who had emigrated to Massachusetts. The consumption of calories, complex carbohydrates, magnesium, and fluoride (from tea) was higher in Ireland, but the proportion of calories derived from total fat, cholesterol and blood pressure levels, and the amount of cigarette smoking did not differ markedly between brothers on different sides of the Atlantic. However, brothers who stayed behind in Ireland led more active lives, expending much more energy at work and at leisure, while weight, skinfold thickness (a measure of body fat), and the number of abnormal electrocardiograms were greater for the Boston brothers. Autopsies showed that the Boston brothers also developed serious atherosclerosis in their coronary arteries and aortas at much earlier ages. One implication of this is more evidence that the amount (or type) of food consumed may be of secondary importance with physically active people.

Numerous studies have found that cholesterol reduction follows disciplined programs of walking and cycling. Observations of men ski-racing in Sweden revealed dramatic drops in blood lipids. Under the auspices of the Netherlands Institute of Nutrition, a group of prisoners increased their expenditure of energy by 560 calories for five days a week and reduced their blood cholesterol an average of 11 mg, even with an extra ration of food and no apparent restriction on dietary fat. Prisoners who used up only 450 calories in extra exercise had reductions of only 5 mg, and then only if their extra ration did not have a high fat content. At the lower level of energy expenditure, higher amounts of saturated fats apparently prevented a decrease in cholesterol levels.

Many studies have focused on the relation of diet and physical activity to blood cholesterol levels in young men. One such experiment, described in the *American Journal of Clinical Nutrition*, used treadmill running to test 86 subjects ranging widely in body weight, muscle condition, and exercise history. The greatest average reduction in blood cholesterol levels occurred in obese men and were independent of dietary and weight changes.

In another study, reported in the *Journal of Lipid Research*, 133 young men participated variously in a ten-week program of cross-country running, golf, tennis, gymnastics, wrestling, and weight-lifting. Not surprisingly, those who volunteered for the most vigorous activity had the biggest decreases in blood cholesterol. The most productive types of exercise, notably running and tennis, involved rapid movements of arms and legs and rapid flexing of muscles. Wrestling and weight-lifting, vigorous enough but described as "static" physical exertion, resulted in little or no detectable changes in cholesterol levels.

Claims have been made that weight lifting is even more effective than running. These claims are based on observations that have only a superficial validity. "Once you've reached a certain level of fitness," notes Dr. Larry Gibbons, the medical director of Dr. Kenneth Cooper's Aerobic Center in Dallas, "your cholesterol levels change much more slowly than if you're starting from being totally out of condition. To compare changes in cholesterol in runners who were already conditioned with weight lifters who started from a deconditioned state is likely to produce questionable results."

It should also be noted that veterans of aerobic exercise programs ("aerobic" denotes a substantially increased and sustained intake of oxygen with cardiovascular benefits) may be quite diet-conscious, limit their consumption of fatty foods, and be less likely to be overweight, smoke, or abuse alcohol.

Although vigorous exercise clearly can benefit the heart, the relationship has some complications. For instance, among 681 former Harvard athletes (letter men), those who had won the most outstanding awards tended to die at a slightly earlier age than the others, and early deaths were more likely to be due to coronary heart disease. This may be a case of stereotypical athletes who let themselves go to pot once their glory days are over, and the greater their peak prowess, the steeper their decline in health.

Other complications were revealed in a study conducted jointly by researchers at the University of North Carolina and the University of Washington and reported in *The New England Journal of Medicine*. The researchers concluded that men who regularly jog, run, chop wood, play squash, or engage in other strenuous exercise do indeed reduce their overall risk of heart attack. But when they do have attacks, their chances of suffering cardiac arrest are greater during workouts than at other times. However, the risk was bound to be much higher for those who exercised infrequently or for less than twenty minutes a week and, overall, the benefits of vigorous exercise for healthy men with no previous history of heart disease outweighed the risks.

Skeptics adamantly opposed to the very idea of aerobic exercise point to the example of the late James Fixx. The foremost American proponent of running, Mr. Fixx dropped dead of a heart attack at 52 while running in Vermont in the summer of 1984. However, it turned out that he had a family background of heart disease (his father had suffered a fatal heart attack at a much younger age), and his own medical record included adverse indications such as high cholesterol, overweight, and hints of possible heart problems. It is plausible that his running and drastic weight loss actually extended his life beyond its actuarially predicted span.

The assertion has been made that *only* such forms of aerobic exercise as swimming, long-distance running, or cross-country skiing significantly elevate the beneficial HDLs, and that other or lesser exertions are ineffective. This contention appears to be too narrow. Exercise need not be conventional to have good effects. For example, thirteen members of the Australian National University Mountaineering Club took part in an eight-week climb in the Himalayas—a truly sustained aerobic venture. The men ranged from 22 to 43 years old. During the eight weeks their body weight did not change significantly, alcohol consumption fell to zero, and only two men smoked (five cigarettes daily). The intake of food increased but consisted mainly of carbohydrates. The men's average HDL concentrations almost doubled within three weeks and remained at that level for the rest of the climb. Although the arduousness of the feat was given much of the credit, exposure to cold, high altitudes, and reduced oxygen in the air may also have played a role.

The Laboratory of Physiological Hygiene of the University of Minnesota's School of Public Health studied the effects of *moderate* exercise on total blood cholesterol, lipoproteins, triglycerides, body weight, and skinfold thickness of a group of sedentary middle-aged

men. All were put on the same controlled-fat diet, but some performed exercise consisting of an hour of walking on a treadmill
three times a week at an average of three miles per hour on a four-
percent uphill grade, while the others did no treadmill-walking.
After a period of twelve weeks the men who had exercised lost more
weight and body fat and had more favorable lipoprotein fractions
than the men who had not exercised. The results suggest that milder
exercise, if regular, also affects blood lipids and increases HDLs.
Loss of weight probably contributed as well.

Finnish researchers also investigated the effects of moderate
physical exercise on blood lipoproteins, recruiting about 100 men
volunteers between the ages of 40 and 45 through local radio and
newspaper advertising. One group did moderate exercise in a four-
month program of three of four weekly sessions; the control group
continued their usual more or less inactive lives. At the end, exer-
cisers had significantly lowered their blood triglycerides and raised
their HDL levels; no changes occurred in the control group. The results imply that mild-to-moderate physical exercise can beneficially
affect blood lipids in healthy middle-aged men and may help to prevent coronary heart disease.

Thus, the data on the relationship between physical training and
lipid/lipoprotein levels in the blood generally, but not always, agree.
Interpretations of any test results must take into account initial cholesterol levels, age, duration and intensity of exercise, and individual weight, proportion of body fat, and aerobic capacity. All can influence the effect of exercise on blood cholesterol and lipoproteins.

We can no longer rationally question whether habitual exercise
is a boon to our hearts. But we can ask, how much and what kind of
exercise? Are morning calisthenics as good for the heart as stretch-
ing the muscles? To achieve cardiovascular benefits must we work
up a sweat in arduous, rhythmic activities that raise the heart rate 30
to 50 beats per minute above its rest condition? If aerobic exercise *is*
best for the heart, how often and how long should we run, swim, or
skip rope? Or is gradually increased brisk walking adequate for
most people, as many authorities contend? Because the answers to

these questions vary with the individual, the best advice is: Yes, exercise. But do so under the guidance of a doctor or other health professional.

It is no longer in contention that exercise tends to be a natural cholesterol-lowering habit. Or that it influences positively lipoprotein fractions. Or that it is a "plus" in the protection of the heart against cardiovascular disease. It should be noted, however, that there may be differences between men and women and that some studies indicate a very strenuous level of exercise is required to bring down total cholesterol levels.

Exercise is no guarantee against death from sudden heart attacks. It cannot eliminate, only help to mitigate, such risk factors as hereditary predisposition. But it can be invigorating and possibly life-extending for *everybody*. Exercise can give a new lease on life even for those whose genes have pre-destined them for fatal heart attacks.

4. Under Stress and Overweight

Stress does not inevitably lead to overweight. But it is so often relieved by compulsive eating and drinking that unwelcome weight gain and stress seem appropriately linked.

Most observers agree that stress raises cholesterol levels. Just how much is hard to determine. Stress is a major coronary heart disease risk factor unto itself. But it is accentuated by its relation to other risk factors such as high blood pressure and inherited personality traits, as well as overeating, smoking, and alcohol or drug abuse.

The personality category known as "Type A" seems to be especially vulnerable to stress and heart attacks. Type A behavior is especially exemplified by feelings of urgency about time—rage at being kept waiting, internal pressure to rush, rush, rush. A Type A person ignores advice from friends and family to slow down; is too impatient to wait for other people to finish their sentences; speaks rapidly, blinks often, grimaces, clenches fists, even pounds on desks. He eats rapidly, sometimes compulsively. Above all, he is fiercely competitive and infuriated at obstacles that stand in the way of his rapid attainment of ambitious goals.

Fortunately, Type A behavior can be modified, even after it may have led to a heart attack. When this stressful, aggressive way of relating to others is brought under control, heart attack victims have a good chance of avoiding a recurrence.

For example, more than 800 men who had suffered heart attacks and changed their Type A ways had only half the usual number of second heart attacks, according to a study by a team from Mount Zion Hospital and Medical Center in San Francisco and Stanford University School of Medicine. They were encouraged and helped to curb their sense of urgency, their competitiveness, their inability to relax, and their easily aroused frustration, suspicion and hostility.

One simple but surprisingly effective technique, popularized by Dr. Herbert Benson in connection with what he has called the Relaxation Response, should be taught to many Type A people (and is worth knowing for anyone faced with stressful times). Every morning and evening, for ten to fifteen minutes, sit quietly, close your eyes, and repeat to yourself with each breath a simple single syllable.

In reducing the stress risk, it is fair to ask if many of these men did not lose weight and lower their blood pressure and cholesterol levels at the same time.

But, in any case, if changing behavior can have such striking rewards for people with certified heart disease, it should be even more helpful for those who have not yet had a heart attack.

Overweight by itself, regardless of a possible stress relation, should be regarded as an independent risk factor—like high blood pressure and smoking—for cardiovascular disease. This was one conclusion of the Framingham Heart Study in a follow-up report made 26 years after the study was begun. The study also strongly suggested that there is a positive correlation between blood cholesterol and body weight as well as diet.

An analysis of the long-term Framingham data, published in *Circulation*, states: "Metropolitan Relative Weight, or percentage of desirable weight, on initial examination predicted 26-year incidence of cardiovascular disease independent of age, cholesterol, systolic blood pressure, cigarettes, left ventricular hypertrophy and glucose tolerance." That is, excess weight at the beginning of the study turned out to mean that heart disease was more likely to appear.

The Zutphen Study, conducted in a small Netherlands town

over a period of more than two decades beginning in 1960, rein-
forced this weight-cholesterol relationship. In randomly selected
40–59-year-old men, average blood cholesterol increased significantly with increases in body weight. A rise in body weight of 1
kilogram (2.2 pounds) was associated with a 2-mg rise in blood
cholesterol. Presumably, then, an overweight person losing 10 kilo-
grams (22 pounds) could expect a 20-mg drop in blood cholesterol.
(Any appreciable loss in weight, of course, is presumed to mean a
reduced intake of fatty, cholesterol-high foods.)

"In a free-living, weight-gaining population of middle-aged
men," the report of the Zutphen Study summarized, "body weight is
the most important determinant of serum cholesterol. Evidence is
also accumulating that in such a population dietary cholesterol is a
determinant of serum cholesterol independent of body weight."

When a disease has multiple risk factors, there are bound to be
interdependencies; come to grips with one factor and you defuse one
or more others. The overweight man with high blood pressure who
trims down may find that both his blood pressure and blood lipids
come down with his weight.

In a Tecumseh, Michigan, study involving some 4000 adults,
the degree of obesity, more than the particulars of diet, correlated
with blood lipid levels, and a majority of the men and women were
overweight by comparison with ideal weights associated with lowest
mortality. One interpretation of this study, reported in the *Journal of
the American Medical Association*, was that weight reduction might
well be the best first step toward controlling excessive blood lipids in
the general population. Because fatty foods contribute more than
any other component of diet to overweight—and to higher blood
cholesterol—any responsible weight reduction program must cut
down drastically on fats.

In the Framingham Study as well, the development of coronary
heart disease in both sexes was tied to relatively heavy body weight.
Other studies found an increasing rate of coronary heart disease
with overweight even in younger men. The American Cancer Society and the Metropolitan Life Insurance Company concur that
overweight increases the risk of early death in general and from coro-

nary heart disease in particular. (Interestingly, though, an American Cancer Society questionnaire asked about weight, height, and smoking but not about dietary habits, blood pressure, and cholesterol.)

The rewards of taking measures to reduce risk factors subject to personal modification were graphically illustrated in a five-to-six-year study of 19,409 Belgian men, sponsored by the World Health Organization. Some of the men, the controls, were told simply to continue their usual lifestyle. The others, the "intervention group," were asked to change all habits that aggravated risk factors for heart disease, for example, to modify diets and to cut down on or stop smoking cigarettes. The result was that the intervention group reduced their blood pressures and cholesterol levels, their overall death rate was 17.5 percent less than for the controls who did not change their ways, and they had 34.5 percent fewer heart attacks.

It is clear that people, especially men, at risk for atherosclerotic heart disease can avoid or delay the onset of severe symptoms by taking sensible action. A likely first priority is the loss of excess weight, aided by eating less fat (and less of the wrong fat) and achieving better management of stress.

5. An Early Start—That Proverbial Ounce of Prevention

As we marvel at the miracles of bypass surgery, heart transplants, and even artificial hearts, may we also not marvel that so little emphasis is put on keeping our hearts from becoming so damaged in the first place that they require radical intervention? "Billions for technology," we might paraphrase Patrick Henry, "but pennies for prevention."

Preventive measures can hardly get under way too soon, since considerable evidence indicates that heart disease begins in earliest childhood. Thickening of blood vessels leading to atherosclerotic plaques has been observed in preschool youngsters. Arteries in some adolescents have narrowed up to 55 percent due to plaque. As noted earlier, an alarming number of young people—particularly males—have detectable atherosclerosis by their early twenties. In countries where coronary heart disease is prevalent, cholesterol levels in the young are also high. Children with high cholesterol grow into adults with high cholesterol.

The high incidence of arterial plaques found in autopsies of American war casualties in both Vietnam and Korea dispels the notion that heart disease is restricted to the unfit or the aging. It also suggested that much of the general population may be affected.

Children who will become "high risk" adults can often be identified from family histories of parents, grandparents, and close relatives. A child's family background of hypercholesterolemia (high blood cholesterol levels), high blood pressure, premature coronary heart disease, or stroke should prompt the doctor to test the child at least twice for blood cholesterol.

Everybody past puberty should be tested for blood lipoprotein levels, in the opinion of Dr. Carlos A. Dujovne, Professor of Medicine and Director of the Lipid-Arteriosclerosis Prevention Clinic of the University of Kansas Medical Center. And the NIH Consensus Development Panel recommended in December 1984 that blood cholesterol levels above 170 mg (75th percentile for ages 2 to 19) in young people should be cause for counseling about diet and other risk factors (obesity, exercise, smoking) and annual examinations. (The "75th percentile" means that 75 percent of 2–19-year-olds have cholesterol levels of 170 mg or less.) Young people with levels over 185 mg (90th percentile) should receive even more intensive dietary instruction and close supervision for other risk factors. Cholesterol levels over 200 mg (95th percentile) were considered a special category with possible hereditary hypercholesterolemia. Young people with such cholesterol levels should have strictly controlled diets. Many can be expected to respond favorably to diet changes alone, but those who do not, it was advised, should be considered for treatment with lipid-lowering medication such as cholestyramine. (Members of the family should also seek medical advice.) Dietary management of young people with elevated blood cholesterol levels should be part of an overall program of regular exercise, maintenance of ideal weight, low salt intake, and no smoking at all.

All students of atherosclerosis agree that the greatest prospect for preventing coronary heart disease lies in discovering and controlling risk factors at the earliest possible age. This is both possible and desirable. Hereditary tendencies toward high blood levels of cholesterol and triglycerides can reportedly even be detected at birth in umbilical cord blood.

Investigations in the Netherlands, where the incidence of coronary heart disease is now alarmingly high, indicated that as many as 30 percent of preschool children have excessive blood lipids. But experiments with families whose members ranged in age from 4 to

91 established that it is possible to lower cholesterol levels at practically any age. Children responded especially well to dietary management. In another example, Australian teenagers on vegetarian diets—extremely restrictive, to be sure—were found to have blood cholesterol levels 30–50 mg lower than their peers on conventional diets. Because changes in blood vessel walls are the culmination of years of plaque build-up, sound dietary habits begun in childhood can be exceptionally beneficial.

In the United States, which also needs to take measures to start children off on the right route to adult health, pediatricians have tended to be too cautious in diet counseling. But change is underway. For example, the 1985 edition of Dr. Spock's *Baby and Child Care* no longer recommends egg yolks—long a staple food of older babies—because of worries about cholesterol. And in Scottsdale, Arizona, a private clinic in cooperation with local health officials has been developing dietary modifications to lower blood cholesterol in school children.

An even more ambitious plan is under way in Jackson County, Michigan, where 24,000 children in elementary grades are participating in a far-reaching program designed to improve the health of their hearts. Called "Feelin' Good," the program combines classroom instruction with aerobic exercise. The children are taught basic concepts of heart health: Get plenty of exercise; eat good food; stay thin; don't smoke; be happy. The result has been that as the children exercise and become more physically fit, they tend to eat much less sugar, cholesterol, and salt than other nonexercising children. Both cholesterol and blood pressures of Feelin' Good children go down significantly, and the children weigh less than their classmates; this is particularly true for the older youngsters.

"In elementary school," observed Charles Kuntzelmen, who developed the program, "four percent of children have elevated blood pressure, nineteen percent carry too much fat, and almost all the kids have tried smoking. And children do experience stress concerning parental difficulties, peer conflict, school sports and illness."

Such early cardiovascular risk factors are being studied in over 5000 children by Dr. Gerald Berenson of the Louisiana State University Medical Center and head of the Bogalusa Heart Study. "We're finding that those risk factors which include high cholesterol as well as obesity and high blood pressure track into adulthood," said Dr. Berenson. "That is, what you see in children predicts what you're going to see in them as adults. If we want to prevent heart disease, we'll have the most success if we begin with children."

Perhaps no one has addressed the subject of preventive health medicine in general better than Derek Bok, President of Harvard University. In "Needed: A New Way to Train Doctors," which appeared in *Harvard Magazine*, May–June 1984, he wrote:

> Medical schools can make more significant contributions along different lines. To begin with, faculties can offer better instruction in preventive medicine. Up to half of all illness in the United States could be avoided through changes in behavior brought about by voluntary adjustments in lifestyle or by preventive measures on the part of the government and private organizations. The latter are primarily the responsibility of the state, acting through appropriate rules and incentives.
>
> But education and persuasion can bring individuals to avoid smoking, excessive drinking, dietary deficiencies, inadequate exercise, unknowing exposure to health hazards, and many other forms of dangerous behavior. In this endeavor, the media and the schools have important roles to play. But physicians have a special competence to discover risks that patients unwittingly run in their daily lives. They also have a special status and authority that can help them persuade individuals to alter their habits.
>
> Yet prevention currently receives only 1.5 percent of the total teaching time in the medical curriculum. One could not exaggerate the impact of more instruction—we know little about the process of changing human behavior. Even so, there is little doubt that doctors could learn to be more effective in detecting avoidable causes of disease, more competent in using epidemiological techniques to identify community measures for prevention, and more adept at persuading patients to minimize needless risks. With a greater number of primary care practitioners and the growth of health maintenance organizations and other community-based institutions for health care, the opportunities for doctors to make such contributions seem destined to increase.

6. Women—The (Relatively) Immune Gender

Why was the study just on men and not on women too?" a female television newscaster asked after the NHLBI findings on cholesterol and heart disease were released early in 1984.

It is a question asked by men as well as women. Why does study after study, in the Scandinavian countries, the United Kingdom, the Netherlands, Japan, Africa, the United States, deal almost exclusively with men? The answer is simply that women of child-bearing age almost never have heart attacks. (Rare exceptions are women with high blood pressure, diabetes, inherent heart defects, or other special medical problems.) Premenopausal women also tend to have low cholesterol levels compared to men.

Although women's relative immunity is evident, the reasons for it are still a mystery. Also, it is not unique to humans. In research on chickens, it was found that hens laying eggs produce tremendous amounts of cholesterol but do not develop atherosclerosis. However, as soon as they grow too old for egg laying, they develop athero-sclerosis very quickly.

Possible links to hormones were suggested by a study of 20–44-year-old women, under the auspices of the National Institutes of Health, to learn the effects of oral contraceptives on cholesterol levels. Women using seven different pills were compared with women who used no oral contraceptives. All seven pills slightly increased blood cholesterol. Pills (Norum, Enovid, and Oracon) with more estrogen (female sex hormone) and less progestin (also called progesterone, a hormone that prepares the uterus to receive a fertilized egg) increased the desirable HDL-cholesterol; only Enovid did not also increase the undesirable LDL-cholesterol. In all cases, the increases in total cholesterol were too small to be of concern to these menstruating women. None of the women taking any of the oral contraceptives had cholesterol levels that suggested an increased risk. (In postmenopausal women between the ages of 45 and 65 who took estrogen, another study found slightly higher HDL-cholesterol and lower LDL-cholesterol levels, but the difference between women who used estrogen and those who did not was not significant.) At least for women of child-bearing age, estrogen seems to be a formidable protective agent against hardening of the arteries.

It has also been suggested that menstruation has a "cleansing effect." The average woman loses about one percent of total blood volume with each menses, or 10 percent or more a year. Menstruation, then, over a period of 35 years, produces about three complete changes of blood, possibly flushing out cholesterol. Only with the cessation of menstruation would women's arteries begin to clog. Then their heart attacks, if they have them, will generally occur at a much older age than the ominous fifties for men.

However, our own (unpublished) studies of chickens cast some doubt on this theory. When hens were given a drug that prevented the laying of fully formed eggs and forced their bodies to reabsorb the egg (with all its cholesterol), the hens still did not develop atherosclerosis. The elimination of cholesterol by laying eggs apparently does not explain the hens' immunity during egg laying, no more than the possible elimination of cholesterol by menstruation explains women's immunity.

After menopause, women can expect no advantages over men. Heredity and lifestyle then affect cholesterol and other risk factors much as they do in men. Moreover, even women with previously low cholesterol levels after menopause may be as vulnerable to coronary heart disease as men.

Heavier smoking and greater stress have traditionally been associated with men. To the extent that this is true, women have been blessed. But according to the latest reports more women are smoking than ever before and may even be smoking more than men (lung cancer is rivaling breast cancer as women's prime menace). Also, as increasing numbers of women work—and ascend corporate ladders—more face work-induced stress. Regrettably, women in lowly jobs also often experience the extreme stress that leads to coronary problems, but without financial reward.

7. Oftener, Slower— and Less—Is Better

Most of us are aware that all other species of the animal kingdom, except domesticated pets, eat not by the clock but when they are hungry. Man alone has become conditioned to "three squares a day" on schedule. ("If it's twelve o'clock, it's lunch time, and I must be hungry.")

This ritualized timing of meals, of course, is practical. It gives structure to our family, workday, and social obligations and keeps us in "sync" with others. But is it natural? Consistent with the precepts of optimum health?

Experienced dieters, taking a lesson from the animals, have learned to deal with hunger pangs by eating more often rather than suffering discomfort waiting for three rigidly scheduled meals. The strategy of eating less at one time but eating oftener may be especially relevant for people at high risk for coronary heart disease.

This was brought out in a study of more than 1000 upper middle-aged men, described in *Lancet*. When the men were grouped according to how often they ate, heart disorders turned up much more frequently among those who ate three or fewer meals per day than among those who ate five or more times a day. The conclusions were that overweight, increased cholesterol levels, and reduced glucose tolerance (that is, the tendency to incur diabetes) were more likely in men who ate "by the clock."

These findings are consistent with the results of a study of 30–50-year-old English engine-drivers. In this study, interestingly, men who ate fewer meals, and often fewer total calories, tended to be more overweight and have higher cholesterol levels than men who ate more frequently, and often more food overall.

Chickens and other animals show similar characteristics. In animal experiments, frequent feedings produced less atherosclerosis than an equal amount of food given in fewer meals. In a somewhat different study on chickens, one group of birds whose quantity of food was mildly restricted, but whose feedings were frequent, had three times the survival rate of a group of birds left free to eat as much and whenever they wanted (they ate more but less often). Moreover, chickens that ate less but more often had a lower incidence of atherosclerosis.

In the lexicon of eating practices, "grazing" has recently acquired a new connotation. It now refers to the activity of humans— mostly the young—who nibble throughout the day. Grazing is commendable—with reservations. It all depends upon what the grazers are nibbling at.

Marcia Seligson summed it up well in *Esquire*, May 1984: "Eating smaller, more frequent meals is healthier and produces a greater weight loss. Because our blood sugar level is then kept stable, ravenous hunger doesn't overtake us. With frequent, small doses of calories, our metabolism works more efficiently, the digestive system is not strained, and our energy does not sag."

The advice is not new. It was drummed into most of us from earliest childhood not to "bolt" our food. Hygiene instructors told us, "Chew thoroughly. Masticate each mouthful thirty-two times before swallowing." Their advice may sometimes have had esthetic rather than health goals, but it was good.

Eating slowly is conducive to eating less—and to savoring it more. Eating slowly allays stress, is beneficial to digestion and circulation, and to the health of the heart.

8. Aging

Our shared destiny is eventual death. If our hearts are spared in our middle years, they will still ultimately stop beating for one reason or another. Cynics quip, "We avoid strokes and heart attacks by going on abominable diet and exercise programs so we'll be free to die of cancer later on."

If the sacrifices really buy time, it is a fair trade. But the long-term NHLBI heart study has been criticized because it urges a low-cholesterol diet and yet reports that the death rates of dieters and nondieters were not very different. This criticism may be unjustified since atherosclerotic plaques accumulate over a period of years, and the intervention in already middle-aged men with high blood cholesterol may have come a little late to expect major differences in death rates from a relatively small-sized sample.

If youths and the middle-aged are persuaded to cut down on cholesterol, what about the elderly? "But my cholesterol count is 304," a 70-year-old man protests to his doctor. "How can you say that's a good level? Isn't the recommended top supposed to be something around 260?" "At your age," the doctor soothes him, "don't worry about cholesterol. Leave that to the younger guys. They're the ones who are ripe for a heart attack."

True, evidence is lacking that high cholesterol levels in people

70 or older are related to coronary artery disease. But very few have looked for such evidence, probably, in part, because of a presumption that anybody with a serious cholesterol problem is likely to have died of a heart attack or stroke before 70. However, enlightened medicine holds that older people are not really that much different from younger people. The principles of good health are universally applicable. Regardless of age, it is important to keep on practicing preventive measures to promote optimum well-being. *The elderly should be as eager as anybody else to keep cholesterol under control.*

Getting a 304-mg blood cholesterol level down to 260 mg (the average for 70-year-olds) is a considerable achievement in itself. But the older person (or anyone else) should not stop there. It doesn't make the best sense to shoot for a goal that merely puts you on a par with other people of the same age and gender. The goal for *all* adults over 30 should be a total cholesterol level of 200 mg or less.

The findings of a long-term study of elderly residents of the Miriam Osborn Memorial Home in Rye, New York, suggest that blood cholesterol levels do increase with age and that they are not particularly influenced by the quality of nutrition or body weight. The menu at the home was revised to increase the ratio of poly-unsaturated to saturated fatty acids in the diet, and corn oil margarine and peanut oil were substituted for animal and hydrogenated vegetable shortening in the preparation of meals. Blood cholesterol levels decreased appreciably for 18 to 24 months, then, curiously, began to rise and returned to their original levels after 26 to 48 months. Increasing the residents' protein intake at the Osborn facility often produced an increase in blood cholesterol.

If diet, and perhaps moderate exercise, fail to reduce blood cholesterol levels in older people, medication may be advisable.

9. Medication and Surgery: Last Resorts

To medicate or not to medicate? No consensus has been reached on if or when it is advisable.

Physicians, as well as the public, have been bewildered by numbers. How much cholesterol is permissible? Even with all the publicity about studies that link cholesterol to heart disease, some doctors are not alarmed by cholesterol levels above 300 mg. If doctor and patient agree that there is too much cholesterol in the patient's bloodstream, how much will changes in diet help? Exercise? A weight-loss program?

The panel of experts convened in December 1984 by the NIH in Bethesda, Maryland, produced the most far-reaching recommendations yet on the subject of cholesterol and heart disease. Now at last there were guidelines to enable American physicians to identify and treat the one-quarter of the population estimated to have a moderate-to-high risk of developing heart disease because of high cholesterol levels. The goals set (a maximum of 180 mg for people under 20 and 200 mg for those over 30) were much lower than any levels previously thought acceptable by doctors or the public and were well below the average for middle-aged Americans. The panel also assigned relative risks to higher cholesterol levels: moderate risk at 200 mg for people in their twenties, 220 mg for those in their thirties, and 240 mg for those over forty; high risk began at 20 mg above these different levels for the three age groups. "By specifying numbers," declared Dr. Daniel Steinberg, Professor of Medicine at the University of California at San Diego and Chairman of the Panel, "we hope to make things happen."

Making things happen means getting moderate-to-high-risk individuals to seek treatment. The primary mode of treatment is diet. Diet recommendations emphasize reducing the comsumption of fats and cholesterol, substituting polyunsaturated for saturated fats, increasing the intake of fresh fruits and vegetables, turning away from fatty to lean cuts of meats and, even more, switching from red meat to poultry and fish.

How much can even the most rigid diet and eating of "benign" foods lower blood cholesterol levels? Best estimates, for the long term, range from 10 to 15 percent. A reading of 240 mg, for example, is likely to be brought down by changes in diet alone to about 204–216 mg. But exceptions abound. Some people have reportedly lowered cholesterol levels by 30 percent or more, and kept them there, just by eating less and improving their customary diet. Overweight people can certainly expect to enhance cholesterol reduction by taking off pounds, and exercise will help even more. So will relaxation techniques that lower stress, if stress is a contributing factor to excess weight and blood cholesterol. As a last resort, there are drugs.

Several lipid-lowering drugs, used singly or in combination, are now available. These include bile-acid sequestrants such as cholestyramine (used in the NHLBI study) and colestipol, nicotinic acid (also called niacin, a B vitamin needed in small amounts for general health but used here in larger doses), probucol, clofibrate, and gemfibrozil. Common aspirin has also been found helpful.

Bile acid sequestrants bind bile acids and lead to their excretion; this, in turn, increases cholesterol conversion (in the liver) to new bile acids. Cholesterol concentrations in liver cells consequently decline, LDL receptors increase, the liver draws more LDL from the blood, and LDL and total cholesterol levels fall. The usual daily dosage is 16–24 g for cholestyramine, 20–25 g for colestipol. Higher doses often increase the desired effect, but some patients respond well to half the standard dose, which is fortunate if they are suffering side effects. Major side effects are constipation and heart-burn, but abdominal pain, gas, bloating, belching, and nausea sometimes occur. Side effects often disappear with prolonged drug use.

Nicotinic acid decreases the synthesis of LDL, thereby reducing both cholesterol and triglycerides. Dosage starts at about 100 mg three times a day and is increased gradually to a range of 3–6 g a day, according to individual tolerance and results. The drug is relatively inexpensive. The major side effect is widening of the outer blood vessels, causing a flushed skin and possible frostbite in cold weather. Flushing often disappears after a few days or can be relieved by small amounts of aspirin. Nicotinic acid may also increase uric acid and affect diabetics' glucose tolerance.

Probucol reduces total cholesterol and LDL by facilitating the clearance of LDL from the blood. It has no effect on VLDL. It does lower HDL levels but mainly the HDL_3 rather than the more protective HDL_2 fraction. Dr. Stephen Young, a research cardiologist at San Diego Veterans Hospital, observed at an American Heart Association Miami Beach meeting in November 1984 that probucol seems to change the LDL structure to make it more easily degraded and excreted. Probucol tends to cause diarrhea and other abdominal discomfort in perhaps 1 out of 10 patients, but usually these symptoms are transient.

Clofibrate blocks the breakdown of fatty tissue into free fatty acids and may also inhibit liver synthesis of cholesterol and triglycerides, resulting in a reduction of VLDL. Clofibrate has been associated with toxicity. Gemfibrozil hinders VLDL secretion, making it a good drug for lowering triglycerides in some patients. Both clofibrate and gemfibrozil raise HDL levels.

Various hormones play an important role in lipid metabolism (physical and chemical processing by the body), mainly estrogens but also thyroid, adrenal, gonadal (ovaries and testicles), and pituitary gland secretions. Thyroid hormones L-thyroxine and D-thyroxine have depressed cholesterol levels in patients with familial hypercholesterolemia (a hereditary condition that causes high cholesterol levels in about 1 in 500 Americans), but cardiotoxicity has been associated with thyroxine; thyronine and triodothyronine increase the metabolic rate and often lower blood cholesterol. (Animal experiments in Japan found THD-341, a drug comparable to L-thyroxine, more potent than most of the other drugs, but it is not on the market in the United States.)

But it seems wisest to consider drugs only after a revised diet, possibly accompanied by exercise and relaxation programs, has been given every chance to bring about the desired results. Many objections to drug-taking in general apply to cholesterol-lowering medication: It can be expensive and may have unpleasant side effects. Side effects that may be tolerable in treating an acute illness of limited duration are far less so in the absence of perceptible symptoms of sickness and the distinct gratification of "feeling better" after taking the medicine. Also, like medications for high blood pressure, cholesterol-lowering drugs cannot safely be discontinued after a target level is reached without the risk of a rebound to the previous condition.

Taking medications for years without letup, possibly several times a day and perhaps with disagreeable side effects, requires a high degree of motivation, patience, and vigilance. It is a considerable challenge to persist, however convinced we are that it is good for us, when it doesn't make its goodness felt.

Circumstances that may force consideration of drugs are: (1) failure to adhere to a prescribed diet; (2) inadequate LDL-lowering response to diet; (3) severe hypercholesterolemia; (4) advanced atherosclerosis; and (5) an unusually high likelihood of coronary heart disease because of other risk factors. The physician will judge the advisability of medication on a case-by-case basis, taking into account the family medical history, the patient's age, the presence of active heart disease, and other risk factors.

Although adherence to a combined drug and diet regimen is sometimes difficult, people at high risk for cardiovascular disease, for example, due to familial hypercholesterolemia, have a strong incentive to make the effort, and indications are that they have much to gain.

Familial hypercholesterolemia (FHC) results from a genetic deficiency of specific cell-surface receptors responsible for removing cholesterol-rich LDL from the system. Untreated, the outlook is poor; half of all hypercholesterolemic men may expect to die from coronary heart disease by the age of 60. In tests of a particular group, diet alone had only minor effects. But when Dr. Peter T.

Kuo, Director of Atherosclerosis Research at Rutgers Medical School, Piscataway, New Jersey, combined a low-cholesterol, low-saturated fats diet with the drugs probucol (trade name Lorelco) and colestipol (Colestid), the result was a dramatic lowering of cholesterol in 45 out of 50 patients by as much as 36.3 percent in total cholesterol and 41.6 percent in LDL.

The bile-acid sequestrants cholestyramine and colestipol are now considered the first line of pharmacological intervention, when diet change alone does not produce an adequate response, and are frequently administered in combination with other drugs, such as probucol. (Cholestyramine and colestipol are also the treatment of choice for FHC heterozygotes.) Dr. Kuo's results are in agreement with those of experiments at the University of Kansas Medical Center, in Kansas City, where probucol added to colestipol reduced cholesterol levels 30–60 percent more than did diet alone. Probucol also tended to relieve the constipation and other side effects of colestipol given by itself.

Probucol was also effective in treating homozygous familial hypercholesterolemia (HFH; homozygous means inherited from both parents, which reinforces the defect), a condition that produces dangerously high cholesterol levels and usually causes death from coronary heart disease before the age of 30. HFH afflicts about one in a million Americans but, for unknown reasons, is more common in white South Africans (1 in 30,000). The South African Lipid Clinic of the Johannesburg Hospital, after disappointing results with cholestyramine, nicotinic acid, and clofibrate, achieved 27-percent reductions in total cholesterol in three months with probucol and a low-fat diet. But diet and drugs are generally ineffective in homozygous FHC probably because of the absence or lower levels of receptors.

Researchers from the University of Chicago Medical School reported that blood cholesterol in patients with advanced atherosclerosis was reduced by 50 percent (to levels of 150 mg) through the combined use of diet (low saturated fat, low cholesterol), niacin and probucol. These low blood cholesterol levels have been maintained successfully for several years by judicious adjustment of the medication to meet the needs of the individual patient.

Clofibrate was effective in treating a rare, hereditary lipid abnormality (Type III hyperlipoproteinemia), but not a high blood cholesterol level alone. A combination of nicotinic acid and clofibrate was tested by the Coronary Drug Project, conducted from 1966 to 1974, on some 8000 male survivors of heart attacks (myocardial infarctions—destruction of heart muscle by blockage of blood supply) from 53 clinical centers throughout the United States. Blood cholesterol levels fell from an average of 250 mg to the 225–230-mg range, and patients treated with nicotinic acid alone had 29 percent fewer nonfatal recurrences than did a control group.

Physicians treating high cholesterol to ward off the *first* heart attack can generally expect better results than achieved by the Coronary Drug Project, whether they prescribe diet alone, lipid-lowering drugs, health counseling, or a combination of these. Apparently, damage to heart muscle from a first attack creates a new relationship between lowering blood lipids and the chance of further complications.

The NIH Consensus Panel has stated: "New compounds that are more effective, economical, and safe for the reduction of blood cholesterol are needed. Development of improved, more palatable, and less expensive bile acid sequestrants also is needed. Similarly, a search for pharmacologic agents that would favorably influence other elements of the atherosclerotic process is highly desirable."

"Elevated cholesterol levels can be lowered reasonably effectively with the cholesterol-lowering drugs now available," Dr. Antonio M. Gotto, Jr., President of the American Heart Association, declared. "However, we need more effective drugs for lowering cholesterol and LDL and we may also see the development of drugs that will raise LDL levels."

An estimated 11 million Americans of all ages whose cholesterol levels are 265 mg or higher are considered by the American Heart Association to be hyperlipidemics and should be under a doctor's care. Many other millions are in a zone of "accelerated risk" because of blood cholesterol levels above 200 mg. If normal is equated with optimal, the normal should be under 200 mg. Increasing numbers of internists, cardiologists, and family practitioners should be counseling the population to exercise, to eat prudently, and perhaps to take medication.

"The identification of high-risk individuals and hyperlipidemia and their aggressive treatment must be given high priorities for practicing physicians," advised Dr. Gotto. He also urged that every American should know his or her cholesterol and high-density lipoprotein levels.

Both the CPPT and the NHLBI Intramural Type II Coronary Intervention Study showed evidence that increasing HDL independently reduces the rate of coronary disease and of lesion progression.

However, some feel that HDL may have been oversold, that a high HDL level does not diminish the risk of a high LDL level. "There is no evidence that by increasing HDL levels through chemical manipulation, it would help the patients," said Dr. Daniel Steinberg of the University of California (San Diego) Department of Medicine. And Dr. Robert W. Wissler of the University of Chicago Specialized Center of Research on Atherosclerosis stated: "HDL molecules in the bloodstream are frequently thought to protect against heart disease if blood levels of LDL are high. However, increasing recent evidence indicates the HDL levels are not nearly so important if the LDL levels are lowered substantially. . . ." In addressing the International Congress of Lipoproteins and Coronary Atherosclerosis in Lugano, Switzerland, in October 1981, Ancel Keys said that in the twenty-six years he had been observing cholesterol levels in a group of men and documenting their diseases and causes of death, he had found no relationship between HDL levels and the occurrence of coronary heart disease.

"We feel strongly that patients with hyperlipidemia should not be ignored by physicians," said Dr. Scott M. Grundy, former Chairman of the American Heart Association's Nutrition Committee. "We had said . . . to physicians that when a patient comes to you, it's your responsibility to know the patient's risk factors, including cholesterol level." But he cautioned that no patient should be diagnosed as having hyperlipidemia without multiple cholesterol tests and a lipoprotein profile.

The remedy for such patients has been diet and, frequently, medication to rid the body of excess cholesterol. Doctors are faced with the task of changing the patient's eating or drinking habits not for a few weeks or months but for a lifetime. What makes this an especially difficult challenge is that the majority of patients are not motivated by painful or annoying symptoms to follow doctors' orders. The physician cannot enforce necessary prescriptions or determine on a day-to-day basis whether a patient is heeding advice. But in the longer term, blood tests and overt symptoms may tell whether the victim of a classic hyperlipidemia is "cooperating."

When all else fails, an alternative is surgery.

Heart surgery is the most radical form of intervention, of course, to be avoided if possible.

What happens after someone at high risk has that heart attack and submits to bypass surgery? What happens, specifically, to postoperative cholesterol levels?

Atherosclerosis generally continues to worsen, and many patients ultimately need a second bypass. "That second operation may be difficult and risky because the tissues are so damaged and scarred," explained Harvard cardiologist Eugene Braunwald. To avoid a second bypass operation, Harvard researchers believe, the first should be put off as long as possible by trying to control symptoms. This is best accomplished with patients who do not have main coronary artery disease and who have only moderate symptoms.

At the Montreal Heart Institute 82 patients who underwent aortocoronary (the aorta artery) bypass surgery were followed for ten years. The findings were not encouraging. New lesions developed in 67 cases—in the grafts, the native vessels, or both. LDL and VLDL levels were higher and HDL levels were lower in the vast majority who developed new disease than in the 15 patients who did not.

For most patients who had bypass surgery, then, this study indicated that atherosclerosis was a progressive disease whose course bore a close relationship to the blood lipoprotein levels.

"In myocardial infarctions occurring before the age of 55," Dr. Carlos A. Dujovne of the University of Kansas Medical Center told physicians at a Stanford University Medical Center symposium in January 1985, "there is almost always an elevated level of cholesterol present in the blood."

At any age, he went on to say, undergoing a coronary artery bypass does not preclude the possibility of reinfarction if measures are not taken to keep the buildup of cholesterol plaques on artery walls under control. "Research has shown there is frequently a faster rate of development of atherosclerosis leading to the progression of heart disease in the bypassed artery."

Efforts must be made in every instance of such radical therapy to monitor postoperative developments. Blood cholesterol must be measured regularly and photographic records made of any changes in the size of arterial plaques and the cardiac diameter.

Heart surgery, if there is one lesson above all to be learned, does not issue a license to let down the guard on diet—particularly the consumption of salt, saturated fats, and cholesterol.

One surgical technique, which may have been insufficiently recognized in the past as a means to achieve a substantial and lasting reduction in cholesterol levels in hypercholesterolemic patients, is ileal bypass. In this procedure, food is routed around the ileum, the small intestine, shortening the alimentary canal. In trials reported in the *American Journal of Clinical Nutrition*, an ileal exclusion at a sufficiently high level may eliminate all effective cholesterol reabsorption. Cholesterol levels fell well below the accepted "normal" values in the United States.

Some adverse results have been reported for the bypass operation. The most severe of these involves liver failure. Among the other problems sometimes encountered are renal stones, risk of osteoporosis, nausea, diarrhea and anemia.

Part Three
The Rutgers Dietary Approach to Living with Cholesterol

1. Eating Your Way to a Healthy Heart

"Here you've just had a nice low-cholesterol, low-cal breakfast of egg white, corn oil, skim milk, lecithin, mono- and diglycerides, propylene glycol monostearate, cellulose and xantha gums; trisodium and triethyl citrate, fortified with thiamin, riboflavin, and vitamin D; decaffeinated coffee and nutritive lactose and soluble saccharin . . . and you're *still* not happy?"

—Woman to husband in a *New Yorker* cartoon by Stan Hunt

The bad news, of course, is to learn that your cholesterol level is too high. It is a message coming home to millions of Americans led to believe that "cholesterol-wise" they were okay.

The good news is that plenty can be done about high total cholesterol or an unfavorable HDL-LDL ratio. No one need feel helpless or assume that the only remedy is medication.

The focus for action, for most people, is dietary reform. We all know we should be eating less fat, and more polyunsaturated fats in relation to saturated fats. We must reduce dietary cholesterol. If overweight is a problem too, we must cut down on calories.

The surest way to resolve cholesterol/weight problems is a well-designed vegetarian diet. The strictest vegetarians do not have elevated cholesterol levels, nor are they overweight. The strictest vegetarians also consume *no* dietary cholesterol whatsoever—*not one milligram*. It is significant that "pure" vegetarians, who subsist largely on plant food, have very little risk of death from cardiovascular disease. Heart attacks, by and large, happen to people who fuel themselves with food that never grew in the Garden of Eden.

It is too late in the anthropological sweep of mankind for all of us to escape any genetic predisposition to hardening of the arteries.

But reducing dietary cholesterol and saturated fats can help prevent that process from accelerating.

Most of us have taken to heart the warning of recent years: "Eat less red meat." Wary of cholesterol and fat, we have gravitated toward a diet of more chicken and fish. We have learned to forgo a steady intake of bacon, sausage, luncheon meats, steaks, chops, hamburgers, and hot dogs.

Also, if we ate and exerted ourselves physically more like our "precivilized" ancestors, most of us will concede, we'd be less vulnerable to modern diseases. Early *Homo sapiens*—before the advent of agriculture about ten millennia ago—lived by hunting and gathering; they fed off roots, nuts, fruits, and the lean meat of wild animals (a far cry from fatty burgers and fries, sugar-ridden soft drinks, chocolate chip cookies, and ice cream). Paleolithic people, according to Emory University researchers writing in the *New England Journal of Medicine*, ate twice as much fiber and calcium as do contemporary Americans, five times the vitamin C, and much less saturated fat. Admittedly, their life spans were shorter, probably because of maladies that medicine now controls, warfare, and the fatal fangs of saber-toothed tigers.

Whole grains, nuts, seeds, fruits, vegetables, and vegetable oils—in short, all foods derived from plants—are cholesterol-free. Eating these foods exclusively would quite surely lower our blood cholesterol levels. But could it provide a balanced diet that contained all the essential nutrients in the Recommended Daily Allowances? The answer is yes.

There are those, the dairy interests among them, who argue that the total absence of milk or milk products in the diet results in a calcium deficiency. But calcium is to be found in many other foods and in considerable amounts in many vegetables, particularly beans and greens. Health agencies and nutrition specialists are revising downward our requirements for protein and demonstrating that certain combinations of vegetables and grains—beans and rice, for example—will provide all the essential amino acids. Also, anyone consuming considerable fruits, vegetables, whole grains, nuts, and seeds assuredly has a diet rich in fiber and complex carbohydrates.

Well and fine. Realistically, though, most of us are not going to become vegetarians. Nor are most of us going to do a 180-degree about-face in the way we have been eating. Is there some middle ground where reasonable caution can mesh with long-cherished preferences? Yes—for most of us.

Question: Which has more cholesterol, beef, chicken, or fish?

Answer: All have essentially the same, about 75 mg per 4-ounce serving. However, the fat and calorie content of various cuts of beef and other meats varies from forbiddingly high to surprisingly modest. A serving of lean round beef, for instance, contains only 29 percent fat and 214 Calories. (See explanation of Calorie on first page of Recipe section.) The fat is saturated, true, but there is less of it than one would get ounce for ounce in such popular foods as stewed chicken or hard cheese.

Dietary cholesterol is as countable as calories. (See Appendix, Table A) Some foods have deceptively low cholesterol counts: a slice of pizza, 13 mg; two slices of crisp bacon, 11 mg; a half cup of ice cream, about 30 mg. The trouble is we have saturated fat, not only cholesterol, to think about.

The following are general guidelines for those who should watch their cholesterol intake but are not at dangerously high risk for heart disease.

Limit consumption of red meats to three times or less a week. Choose lean cuts. Trim away any visible fat *before* cooking. Prepare without added fat.

Avoid processed or luncheon meats, sausages and bacon, and cholesterol-rich organ meats such as liver and kidney.

As an alternate to red meats, eat poultry (preferably without the fat or skin), fish (both fatty and lean), and shellfish. Other excellent sources of protein are dried beans and peas—lentils, kidney beans, chickpeas, tofu (soybean curd).

Eat hard cheeses sparingly. Preferable by far are part-skim mozzarella and ricotta, feta, and low-fat cottage cheeses. (Grated parmesan and romano, which taste best when freshly grated, are all right in small amounts.) Cream cheese is not recommended, but some markets have a synthetic product (made of soybean oil, wheat gluten, egg white, and gelatin) that approximates the appearance, taste, and texture of the real thing. In general, skim or low-fat milk products, including yogurt, are much more desirable than those made with whole milk.

Use butter, lard, cream, and ice cream very sparingly. Rely on vegetable oils—corn, safflower, cottonseed, and soybean—that are high in polyunsaturated fats. Cream substitutes prepared with co-conut or palm oil (both saturated fats) are not advisable. But there are excellent ice cream substitutes (such as Tofutti), made from soybean curd, that are now available in many parts of the country and have no cholesterol at all.

Whole eggs, that heavyweight on the cholesterol roster, should be given the widest berth. A single large egg (approximately 275 mg) can just about exhaust the cholesterol budget for a whole day. All the cholesterol is in the yolks—the whites are "innocent" and can be eaten freely. Egg substitutes free of cholesterol can be used acceptably in many ways in place of real eggs.

Plant foods are not only free of cholesterol but, for the most part, lack fat altogether or are low in fat. Fiber-rich oats, soybeans, barley, carrots, and chickpeas are particularly good for lowering cholesterol. Starchy foods, such as potatoes, pasta, rice, and whole-grain breads and cereals, can be eaten freely, restricted only by ca-loric considerations.

Years ago, the American Heart Association introduced The Prudent Diet. The general advice was not to overeat, to achieve ideal weight through reduction of caloric intake, to eat less salt and sugar. Prudent dieters were advised to consume no more than 300 mg of cholesterol each day, and no more than 30 percent of total calories was to come from fat—10 percent each from saturated, polyunsatu-rated, and monounsaturated fat.

The diet came under considerable attack, much of it from the medical profession itself. Also, the suspicion was widespread among people who had never tried a single "healthy heart" recipe that the diet would be unpalatable.

Interestingly, University of Minnesota investigators set up a product sampling test for physicians attending a five-day continuing medical education conference on family practice. Each day's lunch-eon and snacks were prepared in strict conformity with Prudent Diet guidelines, with special emphasis on increased fiber and reduced fat (particularly saturated fat) and sodium. The doctors were not in-formed of the experiment until the fifth day.

The results, reported in *Preventive Medicine*, were very positive. More than three-quarters of the physicians were "highly encouraged" to recommend The Prudent Diet to their patients. In a random sampling a year later, 98 percent remembered the diet as "somewhat" or "very" palatable, and 72 percent had regularly recommended it to adult patients.

Now, with increasing evidence of the cholesterol threat, the American Heart Association has introduced a new one-diet-in-three-phases for the management of blood fat levels. The diet is outlined in a booklet called "Eating for a Healthy Heart: Dietary Treatment of Hyperlipidemia," available for distribution by physicians and paraprofessionals.

Phase I is virtually The Prudent Diet renamed. It is designed primarily as a preventive approach for people with a cholesterol level higher than average (based on sex and age), a family history of hyperlipidemia, or other coronary heart disease risk factors such as hypertension and a cigarette habit. Cholesterol is restricted to less than 300 mg a day. Expected decrease in blood cholesterol is 6–10 percent, depending on weight loss and previous diet.

Phase II introduces the dieter to meatless alternative sources of protein. It eliminates egg yolks and reduces dietary cholesterol to under 200 mg a day. This phase is advised as initial treatment for individuals with total cholesterol levels over 250 mg or who have not responded to Phase I.

In Phase III only 22 percent of calories come from fat, and the maximum cholesterol allowance is 100 mg daily. This phase is meant to achieve maximum blood cholesterol reduction (15–20 percent) and is tailored for people with total cholesterol levels over 275 mg and/or high LDL levels.

The results of similarly phased diets have been reported by the American Dietetic Association. At their most restrictive—when corn oil was the only fat used, eggs were limited to one a week, and meat was largely replaced by skinless turkey—the diets achieved up to a 29 percent decrease in blood cholesterol.

A panel of the AMA suggested some time ago that the half of the population with higher cholesterol levels than the other half would benefit from dietary reforms. It advised that whole families should observe these restrictions because when one family member has high cholesterol, others may be at risk too. It also pointed out that lowering blood cholesterol should not diminish attention to other high risk factors: hypertension, smoking, stress, lack of exercise, obesity. (All these factors play their part in heart disease, in the imagery of pathologist Richard Minick of New York Hospital-Cornell Medical Center, "like members of an orchestra.")

"The physician has an obligation to promote public health," the AMA panel declared, "and to be supportive of those measures that he believes will reduce the risk of atherosclerotic cardiovascular disease, the chief cause of death in the United States."

For those who have a "cholesterol problem," dietary vigilance must be a life-long priority. But how richly, variously, and pleasurably they can nourish themselves on the foods that are best for health! However, the success of nutritional therapy will always depend not only on the design of the diet but also the degree of compliance.

Dietary change becomes more acceptable when people are educated into the wisdom of it. That at least was the conclusion of the National Diet Heart Study, conducted by the Department of Nutrition of the Harvard School of Public Health. A group of middle-aged men given proper nutritional information during a two-year program quite willingly modified their diets to decrease the consumption of saturated fat and cholesterol and to increase moderately their intake of polyunsaturated fats.

By coming to know the cholesterol values of foods as we do their calories we can create infinite variations on any given menu plan and continue eating interestingly and safely week after week. Also, acceptance of necessary limitations can be promoted by gradualism and substitution—easing by stages into the new regimen and replacing, one by one, favorite but hazardous foods with reasonable and healthful facsimiles.

The Rutgers Dietary Approach does just that.

2. Dining Out Ethnically

All human victory attests that happiness for man—the hungry sinner—
Since Eve ate apples, much depends on dinner.

—Lord Byron

The Rutgers Dietary Approach negates that old maxim for dieters: "If it tastes good, spit it out."

Times have changed.

In the past decade or so, millions have discovered how many foods that taste good also happen to be beneficial and in harmony with any weight-control program. Like fish, poultry, and lean meats. The marvelous kingdom of fresh fruits and vegetables. The heady world of whole grains and cereals, nuts and seeds.

But another truth is that we are eating out more and more, spending about 35 percent of our food dollars in restaurants. Much of this goes to fast food outlets, perilous eating places for anyone who must be especially careful about fat and cholesterol.

True, salad bars are available in some chains. So are "lean" hamburgers. And at least one leading franchiser offers plain chicken sandwiches. But the hottest item on the instant service circuit is now chicken nuggets, which may be almost 60 percent fat. Fortunately, pizza ranks near the top—it is nourishing, rather low in calories, and mozzarella cheese has relatively little fat and cholesterol.

Standard American steakhouses are what they are, and no further comment is needed.

Another trend of the times is an increasing sense of adventure in exploring other cuisines. The exploration can be enjoyable but wariness is advisable if you must watch your diet.

Of all the "foreign" foods we have found to our liking, perhaps the Japanese kitchen earns highest marks for desirable choices. Avoid tempura, which is deep-fried, but one cannot go wrong with sushi, fish, chicken cooked in broth or wrapped in seaweed, steamed vegetables and rice, or noodles. Try, too, the wonderful variety of tofu (bean curd) dishes.

Chinese cookery has often been touted as the healthiest in the world. In the main, it *is* as fortifying as it is delectable. But eggs turn up not only in the banal egg-drop soup and egg rolls, but in fried rice, noodle creations, and lobster and shrimp sauces. Bits of ham are used to flavor many dishes, even otherwise wholesome steamed fish and chicken entrees. Chinese beef, pork, and lamb are lean, to be sure, but the really low-fat offerings are a wide variety of fish, chicken, and vegetable dishes, black bean sauce, hot and sour soup with bean curd, and subgum chow mein. Also, many Chinese restaurants will now provide brown rice for those who prefer it to much less nutritious white rice.

In some larger cities, Indian restaurants have been proliferating like McDonalds. Certain Indian dishes, with a free-wheeling chef, may be hot enough to lift the scalp and induce hyperventilation. Hotness may not necessarily be forbidden, but to avoid fat steer clear of ghee, the clarified butter that graces some of the breads and the ferocious curry sauces. Stick to pancake-like breads (*puri, roti, chapati*) made without eggs or butter. It is also best to make a meal out of tandoori roasted chicken, seafood and *dal* (a lentil sauce), or the pilaf dishes, and a cucumber salad with yogurt dressing (*raita*).

The Mediterranean cuisines of Italy, Greece, and the Middle East are generally meritorious. They emphasize fresh produce and whole-grain foods, and oils rather than butter are used in cooking. Fish, chicken, and veal, good choices, are prominent on Italian menus. Cautious diners will eschew pastas stuffed with whole-milk cheeses and fatty meats and that sinfully delicious but egg-laden *zabaglione*. In Greek food, with its partiality to lamb, the main pitfalls are some soups and meatballs (veal) *à la Grecque* with rich egg sauces.

Going to a French restaurant presents a problem. The temptations are wonderful to contemplate, but dangerous. You may sometimes have to tell yourself that your diet is temporarily "out to lunch." If you keep your determination not to abandon "rules" completely, forget about "nouvelle" cuisine, hailed for its "lightness"— the flour that thickened the sauces of the old cuisine is replaced by reduced cream and butter. But there *are* low-fat hors d'oeuvres like mussels, or meatless vegetable terrines set in aspic. And you might order frog's legs Provençal (sauteed in olive oil with garlic and herbs), grilled Dover sole, or a poached chicken.

As for the restaurants inspired by memories of *Mitteleuropa* (the Iron Curtain countries, Germany, Austria, and Russia), it's a losing proposition. You may have to surrender to the beef goulashes, wiener schnitzels à la Holstein, and chicken Kievs, and vow, never again.

Trendy Tex-Mex restaurants, which celebrate the gustatory wedding of Texas and Mexico, need not be fat-traps. What could be more blameless than *guacamole* (avocado pureed with seasonings and chili sauce), *arroz con pollo* (chicken with rice), snapper *Veracruzano* (fish baked with red and green chili peppers), or refried beans (in vegetable oil)?

Dine out. Be careful. But *relish*!

3. The Rutgers Dietary Approach

The Rutgers Dietary Approach pragmatically reflects the nutritional principles discovered by research on the relationship between diet and cholesterol metabolism:

- It restricts dietary cholesterol.
- It stresses a reduction in total fat consumption.
- It promotes a higher ratio of polyunsaturated to saturated fats.
- It advocates foods high in dietary fiber.
- It favors *complex* over *refined* carbohydrates.
- It emphasizes the value of non-fatty, unprocessed, low- or no-cholesterol foods.
- It underscores the importance of variety in the diet and the use of preferred sources of protein such as low-fat dairy products, legumes (including tofu), poultry, fish, and lean meat.
- It recognizes the need for adequate calcium best satisfied by a variety of vegetables and low-fat dairy products.
- It uses sugar and salt sparingly and favors fresh fruits and vegetables as nature's way of supplying the required sucrose and sodium.

The approach is exemplified by the 7-day meal plan and many recipes that follow in the next sections. The plan and recipes are intended to be tasty, nutritionally balanced, low in cholesterol and fat, and easy to live with. Saturated fats are almost entirely excluded and because people worried about coronary heart disease must often watch their blood pressure as well, sodium content is kept very low.

Each day's menu contains less than 150 mg of cholesterol and approximately 1500 Calories. This restriction on cholesterol is severe enough to meet the needs of those who must cut back most drastically. Other members of the family who are not at risk for heart disease because of elevated blood cholesterol levels should find the meals and snacks palatable and can always make substitutions or supplement the menus with other foods.

The reasonable expectation is that most people following the meal plan will also lose weight as they reduce blood cholesterol levels. (Note that growing children—unless they have an overweight problem—should not be on a calorie-restricted diet.)

Since we believe food is one of life's great pleasures, the recipes include:

- Old favorites in American households, like tuna casserole and cheesecake
- Satisfying breakfasts with French toast, pancakes, granola, or muffins
- Festive entrees that make entertaining on a low-cholesterol diet a breeze, like broiled salmon with baked potato and peas, honey-baked chicken (try it with wild rice), and a truly elegant veal stew
- Dishes that reflect the rich ethnic heritage of America and the cuisines of other cultures, like eggplant salad, stir-fried chicken, Scandinavian fruit soup, and veal marsala
- Luscious, rich-tasting desserts, such as pound cake, cherry pie, banana splits, and meringue kisses
- Convenient foods to pack in a lunch box or take to a picnic, like a turkey club sandwich or a tofu salad
- Generous "goodies" for a midmorning, late afternoon, or bedtime snack, like oatmeal cookies, nuts, popcorn, orange-juice popsicles, and banana milk shakes
- Easy-to-prepare foods for people in a hurry, like pita sandwiches, curried chicken salad, and blended fruit drinks.

Meal Plan

ach day's menu provides less than 150 mg of cholesterol, little or no saturated fats, and approximately 1500 Calories. Italics indicate items for which starred recipes are given in the sections that follow the Meal Plan. (Note: Ounces of solid foods are weight, ounces of liquids are volume, or fluid ounces—1 cup is 8 fluid ounces.)

MONDAY

Breakfast: 6 ounces orange juice; 1 whole wheat muffin with corn oil margarine and strawberry or *orange-apricot marmalade*; decaffeinated coffee with skim milk

10 a.m.: 1 banana

Lunch: 2 ounces sardines in soy oil on rye bread with lettuce, tomato, and onion; radishes on the side; 8 ounces (cup) skim milk; 1 apple for dessert

3 p.m.: 2 *oatmeal cookies* with 4 ounces apple cider

Dinner: ¾ cup onion soup; tossed green salad with vinegar-corn oil dressing; 3 ounces baked, skinned, *honey chicken*; ½ cup peas; 1 baked yam; ½ cup tofu frozen dessert; decaffeinated tea or coffee

Late evening: 1-ounce package of raisins; 8 ounces skim milk

TUESDAY

Breakfast: 4–6 ounces grapefruit juice; ½ cup oatmeal prepared with skim milk; coffee with skim milk

10 a.m.:   1 orange or peach (in season)

Lunch: 2 ounces sliced turkey breast on toasted whole wheat bread with lettuce, tomato, *no-cholesterol mayonnaise*; 4 ounces cranberry juice cocktail; 1 pear; 8 ounces skim milk

3 p.m.:   1 ounce dried apricots

Dinner: ¼ cantaloupe; 3 ounces broiled salmon with 1 baked potato, ½ cup string beans; *avocado salad* (equivalent to ¼ avocado); fresh fruit salad; coffee or tea

Late evening: 1 ounce salt-free, oil-free *almond-raisin mix*

WEDNESDAY

Breakfast: ½ grapefruit; ¼ cup *granola* with skim milk; coffee with skim milk

10 a.m.:   10–12 grapes

Lunch: ½ cup low-fat cottage cheese with ½ cup diced peaches; 5 rye crisp crackers; ½-inch slice of *pound cake*; 8 ounces skim milk

3 p.m.:   1 ounce dried figs or dates

Dinner: 6 ounces tomato juice; 1 cup *sweet-sour lentils with 1 turkey hot dog*, sliced; ½ cup Waldorf salad; ½ cup vanilla or chocolate pudding

Late evening: Carrot and celery sticks; fresh mushrooms; *onion dip*; 8 ounces skim milk

THURSDAY

Breakfast: 2 slices *whole wheat French toast*; ½ cup blueberries or strawberries; coffee with skim milk

10 a.m.:   10 peanuts in shell

Lunch: *Tofu salad* pita sandwich; 8 ounces skim milk; 1 orange

3 p.m.:   ½ ounce halvah candy

Dinner: ½ cup *potato soup*; 6 ounces *tuna casserole*; tossed salad with vinegar-corn oil dressing; ½ cup applesauce; 1 sugar wafer

Late evening: 1 cup low-fat yogurt with ¼ cup fresh fruit

FRIDAY

Breakfast: ¼ melon; ⅔ cup whole wheat cereal sprinkled with wheat germ, ½ cup (4 ounces) skim milk; coffee with skim milk

10 a.m.:   1 ounce dried apple slices

Lunch: Rye bread sandwich with 2 ounces smoked herring, Boston lettuce, tomato, onion, low-fat margarine; 8 ounces skim milk or buttermilk

3 p.m.:   Plums, cherries, tangerine, or other fruits in season

Dinner: ½ cup fruit cocktail in ginger ale; 3 ounces *Chinese-style chicken cutlets* with ½ cup brown rice and 4–5 spears asparagus; *spinach salad*; 1 piece 8" cherry pie (⅙ of pie) with tofu frozen dessert

Late evening: 1 cup popcorn; 8 ounces skim milk

SATURDAY

Breakfast: 3 slices fresh or unsweetened pineapple; mushroom-onion omelet with egg substitute equivalent to 1 egg; 1 slice whole wheat toast; coffee with skim milk

10 a.m.:   1½ ounces *almond-raisin mix*

Lunch: 1 cup *eggplant salad* served on salad greens and tomato slices; ½ pita; 8 ounces skim milk; *2 whole wheat cookies*

3 p.m.:   1 cup cherry soup

Dinner: ½ avocado vinaigrette; 3 ounces broiled mackerel; diced potatoes; ¼ cup lima beans; sliced tomato with sliced onion salad; 1 piece of 10-inch round *cheese-cake* cut into 12 equal pieces

Late evening: Banana split with tofu frozen dessert

SUNDAY

Breakfast: 6 ounces orange juice; 1 whole wheat-bran bagel with 2 ounces low-fat smoked salmon (Scottish), corn oil margarine; decaffeinated coffee with skim milk

10 a.m.: ¼ cup *granola* mix

Lunch: Falafel with pita and cut-up salad; 8 ounce glass of apple cider

3 p.m.: 1 apple, orange, or other fruit in season

Dinner: *Garlic soup*; 3 ounces *veal Marsala* with ½ cup mashed potatoes and ½ cup zucchini; ½ cup frozen raspberries; 2 vanilla wafers; 8 ounces skim milk

Late evening: ½ cup *strawberry sherbet*

Low-Cholesterol Recipes

S tarred recipes are featured in the Meal Plan.
Many recipes call for pregreasing a baking dish or pan with nonstick vegetable cooking spray. It is useful to have a spray can always on hand (but be sure to heed warnings about fire hazards on the label).

The calorie (small c) is a unit of heat from physics and chemistry (approximately the amount required to raise the temperature of one gram of water one degree Centigrade). The Calorie (capital C) is a unit of energy content in nutrition. It equals 1000 calories and is sometimes called the kilocalorie to avoid confusion. In general discussion "calorie" is used. When giving a numerical quantity, it is "Calorie."

MAIN DISHES

HONEY CHICKEN*

3 tablespoons corn oil
½ cup honey
⅓ cup mustard
1 teaspoon curry powder

1 skinned, cut-up 3-pound
   fryer chicken
¼ cup sliced almonds

Preheat oven to 375°F. Mix corn oil with honey, mustard, and curry powder to make sauce. Place chicken parts in single layer in baking dish pregreased with nonstick vegetable cooking spray. Pour sauce over chicken. Spread sliced almonds on top and bake for about 1 hour.

4 servings.
75 mg cholesterol, 410 Calories/serving.

CHINESE-STYLE CHICKEN CUTLETS*

¼ cup corn syrup
¼ cup water
1 tablespoon starch
1 clove garlic, minced
2 tablespoons low-sodium soy
   sauce
2 tablespoons sherry
¼ teaspoon ground ginger
2 tablespoons corn oil

2 whole chicken breasts,
   boned, skinned, cut in
   ½-inch pieces
2 tomatoes, cut in wedges
1 green pepper, cut in ½-inch
   pieces
1 package frozen Chinese
   peapods (or ½ pound
   fresh snow peas)

Place corn syrup, water, starch, garlic, soy sauce, sherry, and ginger in small bowl and stir together. Heat oil over medium-high heat in a large skillet. Add chicken pieces and cook, stirring occasionally, about 3 minutes or until done. Stir in tomatoes, green pepper, and peapods, then add corn syrup mixture from bowl. Bring to boil, stirring constantly, and continue to boil for one minute.

4 servings.
34 mg cholesterol, 268 Calories/serving.

VEAL MARSALA*

1½ pounds thinly cut, trimmed
   veal
1 clove finely chopped or
   pressed garlic
2 tablespoons parsley

1 tablespoon basil
1 small can or ¾ pound fresh
   sliced mushrooms
½ cup Marsala wine

Preheat oven to 325°F. Cut veal into ¾–1-inch squares. Lightly brown in skillet pregreased with nonstick vegetable cooking spray. Add all other ingredients, cover, and cook in oven for about 40–50 minutes.

6 servings.
104 mg cholesterol, 277 Calories/serving.

BEAN CASSOULET

6 cups water
1½ pounds Navy beans
Low-sodium salt to taste
¼ teaspoon pepper
2 cans low-sodium
   condensed chicken
   broth
2 tablespoons corn oil

4 whole cloves
2 bay leaves
3 cloves crushed garlic
½ cup coarsely chopped
   celery leaves
½ teaspoon thyme
1 teaspoon marjoram
1 teaspoon sage

2 tablespoons bacon bits
8 pieces of chicken
4 quartered carrots
3 halved onions

1 can peeled tomatoes
1 pound chicken hot dogs
Chopped parsley

Boil 6 cups water in large kettle. Add beans, salt, and pepper. Cook for 2 minutes. Remove from heat, cover, and let soak for 1 hour. Add broth. Return to boil, cover, and cook for one more hour. Brown chicken parts in skillet greased with corn oil. In a 6-quart casserole, mix beans, cooking liquid, bacon bits, chicken parts, vegetables, herbs, and undrained tomatoes. Cover and bake in oven at 350°F for 1 hour. Add chicken hot dogs cut diagonally in pieces. Bake for another 20–30 minutes or until beans are tender. Garnish with chopped parsley.

8 servings.
68 mg cholesterol, 599 Calories/serving.

POACHED SOLE JULIENNE

1½ pounds of filets of sole
2 cups diced cherry tomatoes
½ zucchini, julienned (cut
    lengthwise in strips)

2 carrots, julienned
2 celery stalks, julienned
1 cup dry white wine
Low-sodium salt to taste

Preheat oven to 350°F. Place filets in baking dish and cover with diced tomatoes, zucchini, carrots, and celery. Pour in wine. Cover and bake for 20–30 minutes or until tender.

4 servings.
138 mg cholesterol, 96 Calories/serving.

SWEET-SOUR LENTILS WITH TURKEY HOT DOGS*

2 cups lentils
6 cups low-sodium chicken
     broth
⅔ cup lemon juice

¾ cup sugar or sugar
     substitute
Low-sodium salt substitute
1 pound turkey hot dogs

Wash and drain lentils. Combine with broth and cook in pressure cooker 20–25 minutes. When lentils are soft, add lemon juice, sugar, and salt. Cook hot dogs separately and, when ready, simmer with lentils for 10 minutes.

5 servings.
38 mg cholesterol, 365 Calories/serving.

BABOOTIE: AFRICAN CURRIED STEW

2 tablespoons corn oil
4 onions, 1 chopped very fine,
     3 coarsely chopped
1 clove garlic, chopped fine
¾ pound ground veal
½ cup rolled oats
2 teaspoons cinnamon
1 pound canned tomatoes,
     preferably in tomato
     puree
2–3 tablespoons curry
     powder
2 tablespoons vinegar
2 slightly overripe bananas,
     sliced

½ cup raisins or currants
1 stalk celery with leaves,
     chopped
2 tart apples, unpeeled,
     cored, chopped fine
2 dried apricots, chopped
     fine (or 2 fresh or canned
     apricots in light syrup,
     chopped)
¼ cup almonds, slivered or
     whole (skins on)
Tomato juice or water for
     thinning
¼ cup parsley, chopped fine
     for garnish

Heat corn oil in large skillet. Add 3 coarsely chopped onions and garlic and sauté over low heat. Mix ground veal, finely chopped onion, rolled oats, and cinnamon and shape into 1-inch-diameter meat balls (makes about 25). Add meatballs to onions and sauté gently until meatballs are brown. Add tomatoes with liquid from can, curry powder, and vinegar and bring to boil over medium heat. Add bananas, raisins, celery, most of the apples (reserve some for garnish), apricots, and almonds. Lower heat and simmer gently, stirring often, for about 20–30 minutes. Thin with tomato juice or water if stew gets very thick. Garnish with chopped apples and parsley. Babootie is excellent served over steamed brown rice.

4–6 servings.
48 mg cholesterol, 490 Calories/serving.

VICTORIOUS VEAL SAUTÉ-STEW

Flour	1 cup vermouth
Sea salt	½ cup water
Pepper, fresh ground	12 small white onions, peeled
2½ pounds veal cut into	4 carrots, scraped and sliced
cubes for stewing	½ cup sliced mushrooms
1 teaspoon paprika	½ cup scallions, chopped
1 teaspoon rosemary	½ cup fresh green peas,
1 teaspoon thyme	cooked

Mix flour, salt, and pepper. Dredge (coat) veal cubes well with mixture and brown on all sides in greased skillet, sprinkling with a little paprika as they cook. Add rosemary, thyme, vermouth, and water, cover, and simmer gently for about 40 minutes. Add white onions and carrots, cover, and simmer again until vegetables are nearly tender and veal is cooked through. For the last few minutes of cooking, add mushrooms and scallions. Finally, add peas with just enough time to be heated before serving. (If the stew is too watery, thicken with all-purpose flour mixed into low-fat yogurt.)

4 servings.
121 mg cholesterol, 302 Calories/serving.

TUNA CASSEROLE*

2 7-ounce cans tuna
2 cups cooked macaroni
1 small can black olives
1 small red pepper, diced
1 small can mushrooms
½ cup low-fat yogurt

½ cup no-cholesterol
    mayonnaise (see recipe)
½ cup chopped nuts
Grated cheese
Fresh bread crumbs

Mix all ingredients (except cheese and bread crumbs) and place in 2-quart baking dish. Sprinkle with mixture of cheese and crumbs. Bake in 350°F oven for ½ hour.

6 servings.
48 mg cholesterol, 343 Calories/serving.

CHICKEN WITH CURRANT SAUCE

2 whole chicken breasts, split,
    skinned, and boned
1 tablespoon corn oil
    margarine
2 tablespoons finely chopped
    onion
2 garlic cloves, minced

½ cup currant jelly
¼ cup raisins
¼ teaspoon dry mustard
¼ teaspoon black pepper
¼ teaspoon rosemary
2 teaspoons cornstarch
2 tablespoons water

Preheat oven to 400°F. Place chicken in 8-inch-square baking dish pregreased with nonstick vegetable cooking spray. Cover and bake about ½ hour, or until tender. While chicken bakes, melt margarine in small saucepan and sauté onion and garlic about 3 minutes. Add currant jelly, raisins, mustard, pepper, and rosemary. Cook until jelly is melted, stirring constantly. Combine cornstarch and water in a small bowl, mix well, and add to saucepan. Cook until thickened, stirring constantly. Pour sauce over baked chicken.

4 servings.
63 mg cholesterol, 336 Calories/serving.

BAKED FISH AMANDINE

1 pound fresh or frozen filets of
    perch or cod
½ teaspoon low-sodium salt
½ teaspoon paprika
⅓ cup chopped blanched
    almonds

2 tablespoons corn oil
1½ tablespoons dry sherry
Dash of lemon juice

Cut fish into serving size pieces. Place fish into baking dish pre-greased with nonstick vegetable cooking spray, sprinkle with salt and paprika, and top with almonds. Sprinkle corn oil evenly over surface of fish. Bake in 350°F oven about 25–30 minutes, or until fish is flaky. Add sherry and lemon juice during the last 10 minutes of cooking.

4 servings.
88 mg cholesterol, 292 Calories/serving.

MEAT BALLS À LA SEOUL WITH STIR-FRIED VEGETABLES

3/4 pound tofu (soybean curd)
3/4 pound ground veal
4 scallions, chopped fine
1 clove garlic, chopped fine
1 tablespoon toasted sesame
    seeds
1/2 teaspoon sugar
1 tablespoon low-sodium soy
    sauce
Dash of cayenne pepper
2 tablespoons pine nuts
4 tablespoons whole wheat
    flour

3 tablespoons sesame oil
2 cups fresh chopped
    vegetables for stir-
    frying—onions, celery,
    green pepper, carrots,
    bok choy, parsley,
    romaine lettuce, or snow
    peas in a combination of
    your choice
1 tablespoon sherry
Chopped parsley for garnish

In a bowl, mix tofu, ground veal, scallions, garlic, sesame seeds, sugar, soy sauce, and cayenne pepper. Shape into walnut-size balls and insert two pine nuts in each ball. Roll balls lightly in flour. Heat sesame oil in skillet or wok, add meat balls, five or six at a time, and sauté over high heat until cooked all the way through (about five minutes). Remove and place on paper towels to drain off excess oil.

Stir-fry vegetables in skillet for 3–5 minutes. Add meat balls and sherry and stir-fry for another minute or two to reheat. Serve over steamed brown rice and garnish with sesame seeds or chopped parsley.

4 servings.
61 mg cholesterol, 428 Calories/serving.

CHICKEN-STUFFED PEPPERS

6 large green peppers
6 medium-size tomatoes, or
    1-pound, 12-ounce can
2 cups cut-up cooked
    chicken
1 cup chopped zucchini
1/4 cup chopped onion
1 tablespoon chopped
    parsley

2 tablespoons chopped red
    pepper
1/4 teaspoon low-sodium salt
1/4 teaspoon oregano
1/8 teaspoon ground black
    pepper
1 cup shredded bran cereal
1/3 cup packaged quick rice
1 15-ounce can tomato sauce

Cut off tops of green peppers and remove seeds. Cook in large pan of boiling water for 5 minutes, drain, and set aside. Prepare stuffing: Chop tomatoes, saving the liquid; in a bowl, combine tomato, tomato liquid, and all remaining ingredients except tomato sauce. Spoon stuffing into green peppers and place peppers in a shallow baking dish, adding enough water to cover bottom. Bake at 350°F for about 30 minutes, or until peppers are just tender. Heat tomato sauce in a small saucepan and pour over peppers when ready to serve.

6 servings.
18 mg cholesterol, 175 Calories/serving.

BEVERAGES

BANANA MILK SHAKE

1 cup skim milk
1 banana, sliced
1 teaspoon honey

1 tablespoon wheat germ
1/2 teaspoon almond extract

Put all ingredients in blender and blend until smooth.

1 serving.
5 mg cholesterol, 249 Calories.

TEETOTALER'S MINT JULEP

1 cup unsweetened apple
   juice
2 sweet eating apples with
   skin, diced
2/3 cup buttermilk
2 tablespoons nonfat dry milk
   powder

1 tablespoon orange juice
   concentrate
1 tablespoon chopped fresh
   mint, or 1 teaspoon mint
   flakes

Put all ingredients in blender and blend for 1 minute.

4 servings.
1 mg cholesterol, 134 Calories/serving.

PEACH FIZZ COCKTAIL

1 cup unsweetened
    pineapple juice
1 cup skim milk
3 fresh peaches with skin,
    diced

1 tablespoon honey
3 tablespoons nonfat dry milk
    powder
2 tablespoons roasted wheat
    germ

Put all ingredients in blender and whip for 2 minutes.

4 servings.
2 mg cholesterol, 124 Calories/serving.

SIDE DISHES

RELISH SUPREME

2 cups cooked brown rice
1 cup canned whole-kernel
    corn
1 cup cooked green peas
½ cup minced onions,
    sautéed lightly
½ cup red pepper, minced
3 tablespoons chopped
    parsley

¼ cup corn oil
¼ cup wine vinegar
¼ teaspoon low-sodium salt
¼ teaspoon garlic powder
¼ teaspoon fresh-ground
    pepper

Combine first six ingredients in a large bowl and mix thoroughly. Add remaining ingredients and toss lightly. Refrigerate until needed.

8 servings.
0 mg cholesterol, 149 Calories/serving.

HEALTHFUL FRIED RICE

4 tablespoons corn oil
5 scallions, cut in ½-inch
    lengths
2 cups finely chopped carrots
    and mushrooms
1 tablespoon chopped fresh
    ginger
1 cup cooked, diced breast of
    chicken (without skin)

4 cups cooked cold brown
    rice
1½ tablespoons low-sodium
    soy sauce
2 teaspoons sugar (optional)
2 tablespoons dry sherry
4 egg whites, lightly beaten

Heat 1 tablespoon corn oil in skillet or wok and stir-fry scallions for ½ minute. Add chopped carrots, mushrooms, and ginger and stir-fry briefly until tender but still firm. Add chicken, heat through, then remove contents from pan.

Add rest of oil to pan and heat until very hot. Add rice, stirring carefully to avoid lumping. After rice is heated through, add vegetable-chicken mixture and stir, blending in soy sauce, sugar, and sherry. Gently fold in egg whites. As soon as they set, remove from heat.

4 servings.
28 mg cholesterol, 409 Calories/serving.

FORTIFYING HOMMUS

½ cup diced onion
2 cloves garlic, minced
1 cup cooked chick peas
    (garbanzos)
3 tablespoons corn or
    safflower oil
2 tablespoons chopped fresh
    spearmint, or 1
    tablespoon crushed dry
    mint leaves (optional)

¼ cup tahini (sesame seed
    butter, available in
    Middle Eastern or
    Oriental groceries)
¼ cup lemon juice

In skillet, sauté onion and garlic in 1 tablespoon of oil until slightly soft. Place in blender with all other ingredients, including remaining oil, and blend until smooth. Delicious as a spread for raw vegetable salads or sandwich filling for pita pockets.

4 servings.
0 mg cholesterol, 400 Calories/serving.

QUICK-BAKED POTATO STRIPS

6 potatoes
2½ tablespoons corn oil
½ teaspoon paprika

⅛ teaspoon pepper
Low-sodium salt to taste

Preheat oven to 450°F. Wash potatoes and cut lengthwise into strips. Mix oil with spices. Dip potato strips into oil mixture, drain excess oil, and place strips on a baking sheet. Bake for 15 minutes.

10 servings.
0 mg cholesterol, 93 Calories/serving.

SWEET AND SOUR MÉLANGE

¼ cup corn or safflower oil
2 cups tofu, diced
2 carrots, scraped and thinly
    sliced
½ cup scallions, chopped
1 tablespoon cornstarch

¼ cup low-sodium soy sauce
8 cherry tomatoes, quartered
1 9-ounce can crushed
    pineapples, drained
½ cup blanched almonds

Heat oil in skillet or wok, then sauté tofu, carrots, and scallions for 3 minutes. Dissolve cornstarch in soy sauce, add to pan, stir, and add tomatoes. Cook for 5 minutes. Add pineapples and almonds and cook for 2 more minutes.

4 servings.
0 mg cholesterol, 357 Calories/serving.

SNACKS AND APPETIZERS

ORANGE JUICE POPSICLES

1 cup skim milk
1 envelope unflavored gelatin
¼ cup honey
1½ cups unsweetened
    orange juice (others, like
    grape, pineapple, apple,
    and cranberry, are also
    good)

1 tablespoon lemon juice
1 egg white

Pour milk into blender, add gelatin and allow to soften for a few minutes, then add remaining ingredients. Blend thoroughly. Pour blended mixture into popsicle molds and insert a popsicle stick into each mold. Freeze until firm. Unmold and store in freezer in a tightly closed plastic bag.

6 popsicles.
Less than 1 mg cholesterol, 94 Calories/popsicle.

ALMOND-RAISIN MIX*

1 pound freshly shelled
    almonds
¾ pound seedless raisins or
    currants

Mix together and store in plastic bag in refrigerator.

30 servings.
0 mg cholesterol, 123 Calories/serving.

AVOCADO WHIP

1 ripe avocado
2 scallions, chopped
⅓ cup mixed nuts, chopped
½ teaspoon low-sodium salt
1 tablespoon lime juice

Combine ingredients in blender at high speed until smooth.

0 mg cholesterol, 643 Calories total.

BREAKFAST DISHES

GRANOLA*

5 cups uncooked rolled oats
1 cup sunflower seeds
1 cup sesame seeds
1 cup wheat germ

1 cup wheat bran
½ cup nonfat dry milk powder
½ cup corn oil
1 cup honey

Blend dry ingredients in a large bowl. In a separate bowl, mix oil and honey. Pour honey-oil mixture over dry ingredients and blend. (If blend is too dry, make and add more of the honey-oil mixture.)

Pour blend onto cookie sheet and bake at 300°F for 35–40 minutes. After cooling, store in glass container in refrigerator.

24 servings.
Less than 1 mg cholesterol, 194 Calories/serving.

WHOLE WHEAT FRENCH TOAST*

Egg substitute equivalent to
    1 egg
1 tablespoon skim milk

2 slices whole wheat bread
Sugar-cinnamon mixture

Combine egg substitute with skim milk. Soak bread slices in mixture. Brown evenly on both sides in a lightly greased frying pan. Sprinkle with sugar-cinnamon mixture.

2 servings.
Less than 1 mg cholesterol, 110 Calories/serving.

POWER PANCAKES

½ cup unbleached flour
¼ cup rolled oats, preferably
    old-fashioned, uncooked
½ tablespoon baking powder

Pinch of low-sodium salt
½ cup skim milk
⅛ cup egg substitute
1 tablespoon vegetable oil

Heat lightly oiled griddle over medium-high gas flame (or preheat electric griddle or skillet to 375°F). Combine dry ingredients in bowl. Add milk, egg substitute, and oil, and stir lightly until dry ingredients are moistened. For each pancake, pour about ¼ cup batter on hot griddle. Turn when tops are covered with bubbles and edges turn brownish. Turn just once.

6 servings, 1 pancake each.
4 mg cholesterol, 94 Calories/serving.

SOUPS

POTATO SOUP*

2 leeks
2 onions
2 tablespoons corn oil
5 potatoes, peeled and sliced

4 cups low-sodium chicken
   broth
1 cup low-fat yogurt
⅛ teaspoon pepper
Low-sodium salt to taste

Chop leeks and onions and sauté in corn oil. Add potatoes and chicken broth. Simmer about 15 minutes until potatoes are tender. Put through blender and add yogurt, pepper, and salt.

10 servings.
2 mg cholesterol, 113 Calories/serving.

GARLIC SOUP*

3 pressed cloves of fresh
   garlic

Potato soup (see recipe) with
   indicated substitutions

Substitute 3 cloves of garlic for the leeks and onions in potato soup recipe and follow other instructions.

12 servings.
2 mg cholesterol, 113 Calories/serving.

MIDNIGHT SUN FRUIT SOUP

1½ quarts water
1 orange with peel, sliced thin
1 lemon with peel, sliced thin
½ cup raisins
½ cup diced pineapple, fresh
    or canned
    (unsweetened)
4 tablespoons honey
2 tablespoons tapioca
¼ teaspoon low-sodium salt
½ cup blueberries
½ cup diced peaches,
    unpeeled
1 cup fresh cherries, pitted
½ cup mandarin orange
    sections
2 tablespoons fresh lemon
    juice
1 teaspoon orange extract
1 teaspoon lemon extract
½ teaspoon cinnamon
½ teaspoon nutmeg
1 cup seedless white grapes

Combine first eight ingredients in large soup kettle and cook 20 minutes. Remove from fire and cool for 10 minutes. Add remaining ingredients, mix thoroughly, and refrigerate. Serve very cold.

8 servings.
0 mg cholesterol, **144** Calories/serving.

EGG DROP SOUP

4 cups low-sodium chicken
    broth
2 scallions, chopped
¼ cup egg substitute

8 cherry tomatoes
2 tablespoons chopped
    parsley

Heat chicken broth in saucepan. Add chopped scallions. Put egg substitute through sieve and add to soup. Slice tomatoes into each of four soup bowls. Pour soup into bowls and sprinkle with parsley.

4 servings.
0 mg cholesterol, 25 Calories/serving.

THE GREATEST BEAN SOUP EVER

1 cup minced red onion
1 cup minced celery
¼ cup corn or other
    vegetable oil
3 cloves garlic, minced
4 quarts water
½ cup dried chick peas
    (garbanzos)
½ cup dried lima beans
½ cup dried pea beans
½ cup dried black beans

2 new potatoes, diced with
    skin
½ cup diced carrots
½ cup barley
1 cup tomato puree
3 tablespoons minced fresh
    parsley
2 tablespoons minced fresh
    dill
1 teaspoon oregano
1 teaspoon rosemary
1 teaspoon celery seed

In a large soup kettle, sauté onion and celery in oil until soft. Add remaining ingredients, cover, and bring to boil. Cook on low flame about 2 hours, or until all beans are tender, stirring occasionally.

8 servings.
0 mg cholesterol, 257 Calories/serving.

CREAMLESS CREAM OF TOMATO SOUP

8 large ripe tomatoes, diced
2 cups water
1 onion, chopped
1 tablespoon honey
6 whole cloves
½ cup shredded carrots
1 clove garlic, minced
2 tablespoons corn oil

¼ cup soy powder
½ cup nonfat dry milk powder
¼ teaspoon oregano
½ teaspoon fresh chopped
    basil, or ¼ teaspoon
    dried basil
½ teaspoon dry mustard
1 cup low-fat plain yogurt

Put all ingredients except yogurt in blender until smooth. Transfer mixture to saucepan and heat slowly. When soup is near boiling point, add yogurt and simmer for 10 minutes.

4 servings.
6 mg cholesterol, 241 Calories/serving.

DIPS, DRESSINGS, AND TOPPINGS

ONION DIP

½ pint low-fat cottage cheese
½ pint low-fat plain yogurt

1 envelope onion soup mix

Mix ingredients thoroughly and refrigerate. Serve with cut-up vegetables (e.g., carrots, celery, broccoli, cauliflower, green pepper, or mushrooms).

4 servings.
6 mg cholesterol, 82 Calories/serving.

PEAR-CASHEW CREAM

1 cup cashews
2 pears, chopped, unpeeled
1 tablespoon vanilla

Pinch of low-sodium salt
4 tablespoons honey
3 tablespoons corn oil

Combine first five ingredients in blender until smooth. Add oil gradually while still blending until mixture thickens. Delectable as topping for cooked cereals in place of milk or cream.

0 mg cholesterol, 1571 Calories total.

ORANGE-APRICOT MARMALADE*

1 cup orange juice,
    unsweetened
⅓ cup pineapple juice,
    unsweetened
2 tablespoons dried orange
    rind

1 teaspoon almond extract
2 tablespoons honey
¾ cup chopped dried apricot
4 tablespoons tapioca

Cook all ingredients together in saucepan until thickened. Cool and refrigerate. Yields about two cups of marmalade.

0 mg cholesterol, 333 Calories/cup.

EASY NO-CHOLESTEROL MAYONNAISE*

⅓ cup egg substitute
¾ teaspoon low-sodium salt
    or salt substitute
½ teaspoon dry mustard

½ teaspoon sugar
¼ teaspoon paprika
2 tablespoons white vinegar
1 cup corn oil

Combine all ingredients, except only half the oil, in blender at medium-high speed until just mixed. Without turning off blender, add remaining oil slowly and steadily. If necessary, use rubber spatula to keep mixture flowing to the blades. Blend until oil is completely incorporated and mixture is smooth and thick.

1½ cups (12 ounces).
0 mg cholesterol, 165 Calories/ounce.

AVOCADO-ALMOND DRESSING-DIP

½ cup almonds
1 cup water
2 avocados, ripe but not
    mushy, peeled
⅓ cup chopped scallions
    (with greens)

2 tablespoons lemon juice
¼ teaspoon freshly grated
    black pepper

Mix almonds and water in blender until smooth. Add avocados, scallions, lemon juice, and pepper. Nutritious mixture is excellent on salt-free crackers, sliced tomatoes, or salads.

0 cholesterol, 724 Calories total.

SALADS

TUNA MOUSSE

1 envelope unflavored gelatin
2 tablespoons lemon juice
½ cup low-sodium chicken
    broth

1 tablespoon chopped
    parsley
1 teaspoon dried dill
1 teaspoon mustard

¼ cup skim milk
½ cup no-cholesterol
    mayonnaise (see recipe)
2 tablespoons minced onion

¼ teaspoon pepper
1 7-ounce can tuna, drained,
    and flaked
½ cup shredded cucumber

Soften gelatin in lemon juice in mixing bowl. Add broth and stir to dissolve gelatin. Add all other ingredients except tuna and cucumber and beat until well mixed. Chill for 30 minutes, or until slightly thickened. Beat until frothy. Fold in tuna and cucumber, place in mold and chill for 3 hours, or until firm. May be served on lettuce leaves and decorated with tomato wedges.

10 servings.
14 mg cholesterol, 72 Calories/serving.

CURRIED CHICKEN CALCUTTA SALAD

2 cantaloupes or honeydew
    melons
2 cups chicken breast,
    cooked and shredded
⅓ cup no-cholesterol
    mayonnaise (see recipe)
1 tablespoon Dijon mustard

1 tablespoon curry powder
2 cups diced celery
2 cups diced mangos
2 tablespoons sesame seeds
Paprika
Parsley, finely chopped

Cut melons into halves and scoop out centers. Mix shredded chicken, mayonnaise, mustard, curry, celery, mangos, and sesame seeds until uniform. Put mixture in cavities of melon halves. Sprinkle with paprika and garnish with parsley.

4 servings.
55 mg cholesterol, 455 Calories/serving.

TOFU SALAD*

1 package tofu
1 minced onion
1 stalk chopped celery
1 tablespoon wheat germ
2 teaspoons garlic powder

2 tablespoons low-fat plain
    yogurt
1 tablespoon no-cholesterol
    mayonnaise (see recipe)

Mash and drain tofu and mix with onion, celery, and wheat germ. Sprinkle with garlic powder and add yogurt and mayonnaise. Mix until well blended.

4 servings.
0.5 mg cholesterol, 104 Calories/serving.

AVOCADO SALAD*

2 ripe (soft) and peeled
    avocados
2 hardboiled egg whites
¼ cup grated onion
1 teaspoon garlic powder
⅛ teaspoon white pepper

2 tablespoons lemon juice
2 tablespoons no-cholesterol
    ¼ cup mayonnaise (see
    recipe)
Dash of low-sodium salt

Mash avocados and egg whites with fork. Add other ingredients and mix thoroughly. Refrigerate before serving.

4 servings.
0 mg cholesterol, 175 Calories/serving.

SPINACH SALAD*

2 quarts washed and well-
    drained spinach leaves
Bacon bits (soy protein)
2 hard-boiled egg whites,
    coarsely chopped
5 scallions, chopped
¾ cup garlic croutons
¼ cup low-fat plain yogurt

2 teaspoons mustard
¼ cup lemon juice
½ cup corn oil
1 tablespoon tarragon
    vinegar
⅛ teaspoon sugar
Freshly ground black pepper
Dash of low-sodium salt

Tear spinach leaves into small pieces and place in salad bowl. Arrange bacon bits, egg whites, scallions, and croutons over the spinach. Combine all other ingredients and mix well to make dressing. Just before serving, or at the table, pour dressing over salad and toss lightly.

8 servings.
0.5 mg cholesterol, 197 Calories/serving.

EGGPLANT SALAD*

1 medium-size eggplant
2 hard-boiled egg whites
1 teaspoon garlic powder
¼ teaspoon pepper

½ green pepper, diced small
3 tablespoons no-cholesterol
    mayonnaise (see recipe)
Dash of low-sodium salt

Wash eggplant and puncture outer skin in several places with fork. Wrap in heavy aluminum foil and place directly on medium gas flame. Turn occasionally while eggplant softens. When it is completely soft, remove from flame, open foil, and cut in half lengthwise. Allow to cool, then scrape softened meat away from skin into a mixing bowl. Mash egg whites and combine with eggplant. Add all other ingredients and mix thoroughly.

5 servings.
0 mg cholesterol, 32 Calories/serving.

PALACE SALAD

2 Delicious or Granny Smith
   apples, chopped but not
   peeled
1 cup chopped celery
1 11-ounce can mandarin
   oranges, drained
1 medium firm banana, diced
½ cup chopped pecans

¼ cup no-cholesterol
   mayonnaise (see recipe)
¼ cup low-fat plain yogurt
1 tablespoon honey
1 teaspoon Dijon mustard
½ teaspoon fresh grated
   ginger, or ¼ teaspoon
   powdered ginger

Mix first five ingredients in a glass salad bowl. Combine the other five for the dressing, pour on salad, and mix thoroughly. Chill. Serve on a bed of romaine lettuce leaves or watercress.

4 servings.
0 mg cholesterol, 358 Calories/serving.

DESSERTS

SCRUMPTIOUS RICE PUDDING

2 cups cooked brown rice
8 ounces egg substitute
2 cups skim milk
¼ teaspoon low-sodium salt
¼ cup brown sugar
½ cup raisins or currants

½ teaspoon fresh grated
   ginger, or ¼ teaspoon
   powdered dry ginger
½ teaspoon nutmeg
1 teaspoon cinnamon
6 teaspoons maple syrup

Preheat oven to 400°F. Coat 1½-quart casserole with nonstick vegetable cooking spray. In casserole, combine all ingredients except nutmeg, cinnamon, and maple syrup. Sprinkle top generously with nutmeg and cinnamon. Put filled casserole into a slightly larger baking dish or cake pan. Pour boiling water into outer pan to as high a level as possible without spilling water into casserole. Place casserole in its water bath into the oven. Bake about 1 hour, stirring occasionally to keep rice and raisins (or currants) from settling to the bottom. When liquid has almost all become like custard in texture, turn off oven and leave pudding inside until ready to serve. Serve hot with ½–1 teaspoon of maple syrup as topping for each serving.

8 servings.
1 mg cholesterol, 153 Calories/serving.

OATMEAL COOKIES*

1 cup sugar
½ cup corn oil
Egg substitute equivalent to
    1 egg
2 tablespoons skim milk

1 teaspoon vanilla
½ teaspoon baking powder
½ teaspoon soda
1 cup uncooked rolled oats
1 cup whole wheat flour

Preheat oven to 350°F. Mix sugar with oil. Add egg substitute, milk, and vanilla and beat until smooth. Sift remaining ingredients together and add to mixture. Mix well. Spoon batter into individual cookies 2 inches apart on a pregreased cookie sheet and bake until light brown.

24 cookies.
Less than 1 mg cholesterol, 104 Calories/cookie.

MERINGUE KISSES

2 egg whites
⅛ teaspoon low-sodium salt
½ cup plus 1 tablespoon
    white sugar

½ teaspoon vanilla
½ teaspoon grated lemon
    rind (optional)
Cinnamon (optional)

Preheat oven to 225°F (low heat). Beat egg whites and salt until stiff peaks form. While continuing to beat, slowly add ½ cup sugar. Beat until thoroughly blended. Fold in tablespoon of sugar, vanilla, and, if desired, lemon rind. Line a cookie sheet with plain heavy brown paper—a grocery bag inside up is ideal (this kind of paper is perfectly safe to use in the oven). Drop mixture by spoonfuls onto paper and dust lightly with cinnamon. Bake for about 1 hour—until kisses are dry inside and hold their shape. Remove kisses from paper with a spatula while still hot.

10 kisses.
0 mg cholesterol, 43 Calories/kiss.

CARROT DELIGHT

½ cup sugar
1 cup finely blended carrots
Egg substitute equivalent to
    1 egg
1 cup skim milk
1 tablespoon lemon juice

1 teaspoon lemon rind
½ cup chopped almonds
2¼ cups whole wheat flour
2 teaspoons baking soda
1 teaspoon baking powder
½ teaspoon low-sodium salt

Preheat oven to 350°F. In mixing bowl, blend together sugar, carrots, egg substitute, skim milk, lemon juice, and lemon rind. Add chopped almonds, then flour, baking soda, baking powder, and salt. Stir until well blended. Place batter in 9-inch baking dish pregreased with nonstick vegetable cooking spray and bake for 25–30 minutes.

10 servings.
Less than 1 mg cholesterol, 184 Calories/serving.

JOHNNY APPLESEED CAKE

3 cups unsweetened apple
    sauce
2 cups rolled oats
2 cups whole wheat flour
1 cup chopped nuts
½ cup wheat germ

½ cup raisins or currants
1 teaspoon cinnamon
1 teaspoon vanilla extract
½ teaspoon allspice
Pinch of low-sodium salt
Confectioners sugar

Mix all ingredients except sugar to form soft, crumbly dough. Press into two 9-inch cake pans, pregreased with nonstick vegetable cooking spray. Bake in medium (350°F) oven for 50 minutes, or until sides and bottom of cake are brown. Remove from oven and let cool for 10 minutes. Turn out of pans onto rack to cool further. Dust with sugar.

12 servings.
0 mg cholesterol, 250 Calories/serving.

APPLE-OAT CAKE

4–5 tart apples
¼ cup water
1 cup corn oil
1 cup nut pieces
1 cup raisins or currants
1 cup wheat germ
2 cups rolled oats

2–2½ cups whole wheat flour
¼ teaspoon low-sodium salt
1 teaspoon cinnamon
½ teaspoon allspice
1 teaspoon vanilla
½ cup dark brown sugar
Confectioners sugar

First make 3 cups applesauce: core and coarsely chop unpeeled apples. Put in saucepan with water. Bring to boil, cover, lower heat, and simmer until pieces are just soft enough to mash. Mix with other ingredients to form soft, crumbly dough. Press into two 9-inch round cake pans, pregreased with nonstick vegetable cooking spray. Bake in medium (350°F) oven for 50 minutes until sides and bottom of cake are brown. Remove from oven and let cool for 10 minutes, then turn out of pans on to rack to cool further. Dust with confectioners sugar.

12 servings.
0 mg cholesterol, 520 Calories/serving.

POUND CAKE*

¾ cup corn oil
1 cup sugar
1 tablespoon almond extract
Egg substitute equivalent to 2 eggs

2 cups sifted cake flour
2 tablespoons baking powder
¼ tablespoon low-sodium salt
¾ cup skim milk

Preheat oven to 375°F. Blend corn oil with sugar and beat until fluffy. Add almond extract and egg substitute and again beat well. Add dry ingredients alternately with milk and blend until smooth. Place batter in 8 × 5-inch loaf pan pregreased with nonstick vegetable cooking spray and bake for about 25 minutes. After cooling, loosen edges with a spatula and remove from pan. Top with icing, or slice and fill.

12 servings.
Less than 1 mg cholesterol, 254 Calories/serving.

STRAWBERRY SHERBET*

½ cup water
2 tablespoons orange juice
1 tablespoon lemon juice

½ cup sugar
½ cup nonfat milk powder
1 pint washed strawberries

Mix and beat water, orange juice, lemon juice, sugar, and milk powder. Puree strawberries in blender. Blend strawberries with sugar-milk mixture until smooth. Freeze in bowl or plastic container.

6 servings.
1 mg cholesterol, 122 Calories/serving.

CHEESECAKE*

Crust
1½ cups ground graham
    crackers
¼ cup sugar
1 teaspoon cinnamon
4 tablespoons corn oil

Filling
2¼ pounds low-fat, dry
    cottage or farmer's
    cheese
1½ cups sugar
6 egg whites
Egg substitute equivalent to
    6 eggs
1½ cups skim milk
⅜ cup flour
Juice and rind of 1 lemon
⅛ teaspoon low-sodium salt

Preheat oven to 325°F. Combine crust ingredients and pat into 10-inch springform. Blend filling ingredients in blender until smooth and pour onto crust. Bake for 1 hour. Let cool in oven.

12 servings.
2 mg cholesterol, 220 Calories/serving.

WHOLE WHEAT COOKIES*

2 cups whole wheat flour
1½ teaspoons baking powder
¾ cup white sugar
⅓ cup corn oil
3 egg whites

½ teaspoon almond or lemon
  extract
1 teaspoon vanilla extract
1 teaspoon grated orange
  peel

Preheat oven to 375°F. Mix flour and baking powder in small bowl. In a large bowl, blend sugar with corn oil and add egg whites one at a time, blending well after each addition. Add flavors and dry ingredients and stir until batter is smooth. Place teaspoonfuls of dough (one per cookie) 2 inches apart on cookie sheet pregreased with nonstick cooking spray. Bake for 10–15 minutes.

40–50 cookies.
0 mg cholesterol, 56 Calories/cookie.

WISE SUBSTITUTIONS

Instead of:	Try:
Whole eggs	Egg whites (2 per egg), or egg substitutes (2 oz. per egg)
Ice cream, ice milk	Tofu frozen dessert
Whole milk	Low-fat or skim milk
Sour cream	Low-fat yogurt
Luncheon meats	Chicken or turkey breast (skinless)
Butter	Margarine or, for cooking, vegetable oils
Candy bars	Granola
Bacon and eggs	Oatmeal
Sirloin or T-bone steak	Flank or pepper steak, or lean ground beef
Creamed cottage cheese	Low-fat cottage or farmer's cheese
Cheesecake	Angel-food cake; cheesecake recipe, p. 170
Heavy cream	Evaporated, skim, or low-fat milk
Pies or puddings	Bran muffins or meringues
Hard cheeses (cheddar, Muenster, Swiss)	Part-skim ricotta or mozzarella cheese
Croissants, brioches, or sandwich buns	Whole wheat bread or pita pockets
Chili con carne	Meatless chili with beans
Deep-fried chicken	Stir-fried chicken with vegetables
Ice cream cones	Fruit juice popsicles
Tuna packed in oil	Tuna packed in water
Beef frankfurters	Chicken frankfurters
French fries	Baked potatoes
Frying foods in fat	Sautéeing in skillet with nonstick vegetable cooking spray
Canned gravies	Homemade gravies, skimmed of fat
Mayonnaise	Yogurt mixed with mustard, lemon juice, herbs, and spices; no-cholesterol mayonnaise, p. 160
Potato chips or pretzels	Popcorn with a sprinkling of grated Parmesan cheese
Vegetables cooked or coated with butter	Vegetables steamed and seasoned with herbs

Instead of:	Try:
Hamburgers	Chickenburgers or turkeyburgers
Fatty, salty crackers	Wheat thins, melba toast, or breadsticks
Poaching meats, fish, or poultry in cream sauce	Poaching in vegetable stock
Omelet or quiche	Chef's salad or avocado stuffed with crabmeat
Chocolate chip cookies	Oatmeal or whole wheat cookies, or meringue kisses

SOME FOODS THAT CONTAIN WHOLE EGGS OR EGG YOLKS

Batters for french frying
Breads, rolls, muffins
Breaded food
Caesar's salad
Cakes (especially sponge, pound, and cheesecake)
Candy
Cookies
Croissants and brioches
Custards
Danish pastry and doughnuts
Fish (and seafood) cakes
Fish and seafood sauces
Fritters and croquettes
Frostings
French toast

Hollandaise sauce
Ice cream
Mayonnaise
Meat loaf
Milk shakes and malted milks
Omelets
Pastas
Pancakes
Pies
Puddings
Quiche
Salad dressings (some)
Sauces for meat (Bearnaise, etc.)
Soufflés
Soups (some)
Waffles

A SHOPPING LIST

Dairy Case and Frozen Foods

Egg substitute
Skim milk
Low-fat yogurt
Low-fat cottage cheese
Skim-milk mozzarella, ricotta,
  farmer, and parmesan cheeses
Corn oil margarine

Tofu (soybean curd)
Tofu frozen dessert (cholesterol-
  and fat-free ice cream)
Orange juice popsicles
Frozen fruit (no sugar or syrup)
Frozen vegetables (no sauces or
  butter)

Vegetables and Fruits

Enjoy what's in season, but be particularly hospitable to:

Lettuce: romaine, escarole,
  chicory
Broccoli
Spinach and kale
Peppers (red more nutritious than
  green)
Tomatoes
Celery
Onions, all kinds
Mushrooms
Green beans
Green peas
Lima beans
Parsley
Potatoes
Sweet potatoes, yams
Carrots
Cabbage, red and green
Squash, all kinds
Corn
Greens (mustard, dandelion,
  watercress, arugala)

Garlic
Sprouts (bean, alfalfa)
Oriental: snow peas, water
  chestnuts, Chinese (Napa) cabbage, bok choy

Apples
Pears
Oranges
Bananas
Lemons
Grapefruit
Grapes
Avocados
Peaches
Apricots
Melons
Berries
Cranberries
Mangos and papayas
Figs and dates
Rhubarb

Meat and Fish Counter

Chicken, especially skinless
   chicken breast
Turkey, especially skinless turkey
   breast and ground turkey
Veal
Lean cuts of beef, pork, lamb
Fresh fish

Mussels
Clams
Oysters
Crab
Lobster

Grains and Dry Staples

Whole grains: millet, barley, buck-
   wheat groats (kasha), cracked
   wheat (bulgur)
Rolled oats
Whole wheat, soy, and rye flour
Dried beans, lentils, peas
Brown rice, rice cakes

Sesame and sunflower seeds
Rye crisps
Whole grain crackers
Dried fruits
Nuts
Raisins

Oils

Corn oil
Safflower oil
Sesame oil
Peanut oil

Soybean oil
Cottonseed oil
Nonstick cooking spray
Olive Oil

Canned and Preserved Foods

Tuna (in water)
Salmon
Sardines (in soy oil, tomato sauce,
   or water)
Soybeans
Chick peas (garbanzos)
Tomatoes (especially Italian
   varieties, usually very low in
   sodium)

Mandarin oranges
Kidney, pinto, and black beans
Pineapple in its own juice,
   unsweetened
Apple sauce, unsweetened
Peanut butter, fresh ground and
   without additives

Appendix

TABLE 1: CHOLESTEROL CONTENT
OF COMMON FOODS

	Serving Size	Cholesterol (mg)
Egg, large		
Whole	1	274
Yolk	1	274
Scrambled with milk and fat	1	287
Milk, fluid		
Whole	1 cup	34
Nonfat, skim	1 cup	5
Cheese		
American	1 ounce	27
Blue or Roquefort	1 ounce	24
Camembert	1 ounce	20
Cheddar	1 ounce	30
Cottage, creamed	1 cup	34
Cottage, low-fat	1 cup	10
Cream	1 ounce	31
Feta	1 ounce	16

Table 1 (*continued*)

	Serving Size	Cholesterol (mg)
Mozzarella	1 ounce	18
Muenster	1 ounce	25
Ricotta (part skim)	1 ounce	9
Swiss	1 ounce	28
Cream		
Half-and-half	1 cup	105
	1 tablespoon	6
Heavy	1 cup	370
	1 tablespoon	21
Meat		
Beef		
Lean	3 ounces	56
Frankfurter	1	27
Liver	3 ounces	372
Kidney	3 ounces	315
Pork		
Lean	3 ounces	80
Chop	3.5 ounces	90
Ham, boiled	2 ounces	51
Ham, roasted	3 ounces	80
Bacon, crisp	2 slices	11
Lamb		
Loin chop, lean	3 ounces	85
Veal		
Cutlet or roast	3 ounces	84
Poultry		
Chicken		
Dark meat, no skin	3 ounces	82
Light meat, no skin	3 ounces	66
Breast, half,		
fried with bone	3.3 ounces	74
Turkey		
Dark meat, no skin	3 ounces	86
White meat, no skin	3 ounces	65
Fish and shellfish		
Bluefish	3 ounces	63
Clams, raw	3 ounces	43
Crabmeat	3 ounces	85
Flounder	3 ounces	59

	Serving Size	Cholesterol (mg)
Haddock	3 ounces	42
Lobster	3 ounces	71
Mackerel	3 ounces	84
Ocean perch	3 ounces	63
Oysters, raw	3 ounces	42
Salmon, pink, canned	3 ounces	34
Sardines	3 ounces	85
Scallops	3 ounces	45
Shad	3 ounces	45
Shrimp	3 ounces	126
Swordfish	3 ounces	63
Tuna	3 ounces	55
Butter	1 tablespoon	31
Lard	1 tablespoon	12
Buttermilk	1 cup	9
Chocolate milk, low-fat	1 cup	20
Cocoa	1 cup	35
Custard, baked	1 cup	278
Ice cream		
Regular (about		
10 percent fat)	½ cup	29
Rich (about 16 percent fat)	½ cup	44
Yogurt, low-fat	1 container	11
Pizza, with cheese	1 slice	13
Potatoes, french fried	10 strips	6
Brownies	1	13
Pancakes	7 ounces (with tablespoon butter)	54
Noodles, egg	1 cup	50
Cakes		
Sponge	1 slice	162
Pound	1 slice	68
Chocolate cupcake	1	17
Cornbread	1 ounce	58
Muffin, plain	1	21
Doughnuts	1	10
Chili (with beef)	1 cup	28
Mayonnaise	1 tablespoon	8

SOURCES: Feeley, R. M. et al., "Cholesterol Content of Foods," *Journal of American Dietetic Association* 61 (1972): 134, and Weihrauch, J. L., Provisional Table on the Fatty Acid and Cholesterol Content of Selected Foods. United States Department of Agriculture, Human Nutrition Information Service, March 1984.

TABLE 2: CHOLESTEROL CONTENT OF FAST FOODS

(BC)—Burger Chef (BK)—Burger King (MD)—McDonald's

Item (Company)	Calories	Cholesterol (mg)
	Per serving	
Hamburger (BC)	235	32
(BK)	270	40
(MD)	250	33
Big Shef (BC)	470	75
Super Shef (BC)	529	93
Double Beef hamburger (BK)	377	91
Quarter Pounder (MD)	420	77
Whopper (BK)	483	88
Whopper Jr. (BK)	283	42
Double Beef Whopper (BK)	662	175
Cheeseburger (BC)	285	44
(BK)	327	60
(MD)	321	50
Double cheeseburger (BC)	427	94
Double Beef cheeseburger (BK)	478	111
Whopper with cheese (BK)	589	122
Double Beef Whopper with cheese (BK)	785	223
Big Mac (MD)	425	72
Quarter Pounder with cheese (MD)	559	110
Skipper's Treat (BC)	356	58
Whaler (BK)	470	92
Whaler with cheese (BK)	602	122
Filet-O-Fish (MD)	447	61
Yumbo (BK)	381	69
Rancher, beef (BC)	716	118
Mariner (BC)	663	94
Scrambled eggs (MD)	232	366
Hot cakes, with butter, no syrup (MD)	314	47
English muffin, with butter (MD)	178	12
Egg McMuffin (MD)	332	248
Sausage sandwich (MD)	351	54
Apple pie (BK)	238	3
Apple pie (MD)	287	17
Cherry pie (MD)	261	13
Apple turnover (BC)	269	5
Lemon turnover (BC)	282	8
McDonaldland cookies (MD)	278	11
Vanilla shake (BC)	259	34

(BC)—Burger Chef (BK)—Burger King (MD)—McDonald's

Item (Company)	Calories	Cholesterol (mg)
	Per serving	
(BK)	271	31
(MD)	305	25
Chocolate Shake (BC)	352	37
(BK)	298	38
(MD)	340	28
Strawberry Shake (BC)	343	36
(BK)	277	29
(MD)	327	28
French fries (BC)	260	13
(BK)	254	12
(MD)	238	12
Onion Rings (BK)	140	4

Source: "Scientists Tell Their Findings on 'Fast Foods'," U.S. Department of Agriculture News Feature, 1980.

TABLE 3: PECTIN CONTENT OF COMMON FOODS

	Amount (grams per 100 grams[1] edible portion)
Fruits	
Apple	0.6
Apricots	1.0
Boysenberries	0.3
Cherries (eating)	0.3
Lemon	3.0
Melon (Cantaloupe)	0.3
Orange (composite values)	1.3
Peaches	0.7
Pears	
Anjou	0.7
Bartlett	0.6
Bosc	0.6
Plums	
Italian prunes	0.9
Sweet	1.0
Sour	1.0
Prunes, uncooked	0.9
Raisins, Thompson seedless	1.0
Raspberries	0.8
Tomatoes	0.3
Seedless pulp	0.5
Watermelon	0.1
Vegetables	
Snap beans, fresh	0.5
Carrots, raw	0.9
Onions, raw	0.6
Radishes	0.4
Sweet potato, raw	2.2
Miscellaneous	
Carob bean pod	1.4

NOTE: Adapted from Table 1 in M. G. Hardinge, J. B. Swarner, and H. Crooks, "Carbo-hydrates in Foods." Reprinted by permission from *Journal of the American Dietetic Association* 46 (1965): 197.
[1] 100 grams is close to 3½ ounces.

TABLE 4: LINOLEIC ACID CONTENT OF SELECTED FATS

Fats	Linoleic Acid (grams per cup)
Corn oil	116
Cottonseed oil	109
Olive oil	15
Peanut oil	63
Safflower oil	157
Sesame oil	92
Soybean oil	113
Margarine (regular)	50
Margarine (soft)	71
Butter	6

SOURCE: C. F. Adams, *Nutritive Value of American Foods*, Agriculture Handbook No. 456 (Washington, D.C.: Agricultural Research Service, United States Department of Agriculture, 1975).

TABLE 5: RECOMMENDED FOODS AND FOODS TO BE AVOIDED

Every day, select foods from each of the basic food groups in lists 1–5, and follow the recommendations for number and size of servings.

1. Meat, Poultry, Fish, Dried Beans, and Peas
Nuts • Eggs
1 serving . . . 3–4 ounces of cooked meat or fish (not including bone or fat) or 3–4 ounces of a vegetable listed here.
Use 2 or more servings (a total of 6–8 ounces) daily.

Recommended

Chicken • turkey • veal • fish • in most of your meat meals for the week.
Shellfish: clams • crab • lobster • oysters • scallops.
Use a 4-ounce serving as a substitute for meat.
Beef • lamb • pork • ham • less frequently.
Choose lean ground meat and lean cuts of meat • trim all visible fat
    before cooking • bake, broil, roast, or stew so that you can discard the
    fat which cooks out of the meat.
Nuts and dried beans and peas: Kidney beans • lima beans • baked
    beans • lentils • chick peas (garbanzos) • split peas • are high in vege-
    table protein and may be used in place of meat occasionally.
Egg whites as desired.

Avoid or Use Sparingly

Duck • goose
Shrimp is moderately high in cholesterol. Use a 4-ounce serving in a meat
    meal no more than once a week.
Heavily marbled and fatty meats • spare ribs • mutton • frankfurters • sau-
    sages • fatty hamburgers • bacon • luncheon meats.
Organ meats: liver • kidney • heart • sweetbreads • are very high in choles-
    terol. Because liver is very rich in vitamins and iron, it should not be
    eliminated from the diet completely. Use a 4-ounce serving in a meat
    meal no more than once a week.
Egg yolks: limit to 3 per week including eggs used in cooking.
Cakes, batters, sauces, and other foods containing egg yolks.

2. Vegetables and Fruit (fresh, frozen, or canned)
1 serving . . . ½ cup.
Use at least 4 servings daily.

Table 5 (*continued*)

Recommended

One serving should be a source of Vitamin C: Broccoli • cabbage (raw) • tomatoes.

Berries • cantaloupe • grapefruit (or juice) • mango • melon • orange (or juice) • papaya • strawberries • tangerines.

One serving should be a source of Vitamin A—dark green leafy or yellow vegetables, or yellow fruits: broccoli • carrots • chard • chicory • escarole • greens (beet, collard, dandelion, mustard, turnip) • kale • peas • rutabagas • spinach • string beans • sweet potatoes and yams • watercress • winter squash • yellow corn.

Apricots • cantaloupe • mango • papaya.

Other vegetables and fruits are also very nutritious; they should be eaten in salads, main dishes, snacks, and desserts, in addition to the recommended daily allowances of high vitamin A and C vegetables and fruits.

Avoid or Use Sparingly

If you must limit your calories, use vegetables such as potatoes, corn, or lima beans sparingly. To add variety to your diet, one serving (½ cup) of any one of these may be substituted for one serving of bread or cereals.

3. Bread and Cereals (whole grain, enriched, or restored)

1 serving of bread . . . 1 slice.
1 serving of cereal . . . ½ cup, cooked; 1 cup, cold, with skimmed milk.
Use at least 4 servings daily.

Recommended

Breads made with a minimum of saturated fat: White enriched (including raisin bread) • whole wheat • English muffins • French bread • Italian bread • oatmeal bread • pumpernickel • rye bread.

Biscuits, muffins, and griddle cakes made at home, using an allowed liquid oil as shortening.

Cereal (hot and cold) • rice • melba toast • matzo • pretzels.

Pasta: macaroni • noodles (except egg noodles) • spaghetti.

Avoid or Use Sparingly

Butter rolls • commercial biscuits, muffins, donuts, sweet rolls, cakes, crackers • egg bread, cheese bread • commercial mixes containing dried eggs and whole milk.

Table 5 (*continued*)

4. Milk Products
1 serving . . . 8 ounces (1 cup).
Buy only skimmed milk that has been fortified with Vitamins A and D.
Daily servings: Children up to 12 . . . 3 or more cups.
Teenagers . . . 4 or more cups.
Adults . . . 2 or more cups.

Recommended

Milk products that are low in dairy fats: Fortified skimmed (non-fat) milk
and fortified skimmed milk powder • low-fat milk. The label on the container should show that the milk is fortified with Vitamins A and D. The
word "fortified" alone is not enough.
Buttermilk made from skimmed milk • yogurt made from skimmed milk •
canned evaporated skimmed milk • cocoa made with low-fat milk.
Cheeses made from skimmed or partially skimmed milk, such as cottage
cheese, creamed or uncreamed (uncreamed, preferably) • farmer's,
baker's, or hoop cheese • mozarella and sapsago cheeses. Processed
modified fat cheeses (skimmed milk and polyunsaturated fat).

Avoid or Use Sparingly

Whole milk and whole milk products: Chocolate milk • canned whole milk
• ice cream • all creams including sour, half and half, whipped • whole
milk yogurt.
Non-dairy cream substitutes (usually contain coconut oil which is very
high in saturated fat).
Cheeses made from cream or whole milk.
Butter.

5. Fats and Oils (polyunsaturated)
An individual allowance should include about 2–4 tablespoons daily (depending on how many calories you can afford) in the form of margarine, salad dressing, and shortening.

Recommended

Margarines, liquid oil shortenings, salad dressings and mayonnaise containing any of these polyunsaturated vegetable oils:
Corn oil • cottonseed oil • safflower oil • sesame seed oil • soybean oil •
sunflower seed oil.
Margarines and other products high in polyunsaturates can usually be
identified by their label, which lists a recommended liquid vegetable oil
as the first ingredient, and one or more partially hydrogenated vegetable oils as additional ingredients.

Table 5 (*continued*)

Diet margarines are low in calories because they are low in fat. Therefore it takes twice as much diet margarine to supply the polyunsaturates contained in a recommended margarine.

Avoid or Use Sparingly

Solid fats and shortenings:
Butter • lard • salt pork fat • meat fat • completely hydrogenated margarines and vegetable shortenings • products containing coconut oil.
Peanut oil and olive oil may be used occasionally for flavor, but they are low in polyunsaturates and do not take the place of the recommended oils.

6. Desserts, Beverages, Snacks, and Condiments

The foods on this list are acceptable because they are low in saturated fat and cholesterol. If you have eaten your daily allowance from the first five lists, however, these foods will be in excess of your nutritional needs, and many of them also may exceed your calorie limits for maintaining a desirable weight. If you must limit your calories limit your portions of the foods on this list as well.

Moderation should be observed especially in the use of alcoholic drinks, ice milk, sherbet, sweets, and bottled drinks.

Acceptable

Low in calories or no calories
Fresh fruit and fruit canned without sugar • tea, coffee (no cream), cocoa powder • water ices • gelatin • fruit whip • puddings made with non-fat milk • low calorie drinks • vinegar, mustard, ketchup, herbs, spices.
High in calories
Frozen or canned fruit with sugar added • jelly, jam, marmalade, honey • pure sugar candy such as gum drops, hard candy, mint patties (not chocolate) • imitation ice cream made with safflower oil • cakes, pies, cookies, and puddings made with polyunsaturated fat in place of solid shortening • angel food cake • nuts, especially walnuts • peanut butter • bottled drinks • fruit drinks • ice milk • sherbet • wine, beer, whiskey.

Avoid or Use Sparingly

Coconut and coconut oil • commercial cakes, pies, cookies, and mixes • frozen cream pies • commercially fried foods such as potato chips and other deep fried snacks • whole milk • puddings • chocolate pudding (high in cocoa butter and therefore high in saturated fat) • ice cream.

Notes

The following notes are keyed to the text by page number and a quotation from the lines they refer to. Running heads at the top of each page of notes are a quick guide to the location of the referenced pages.

PART ONE, CHAPTER 1. THE DEADLY C-FACTOR

7   "NHLBI announced the results":
     Lipid Research Clinics Program, "The lipid research clinics coronary primary prevention trial results: I. Reduction in incidence of coronary heart disease. II. The relationship of reduction in incidence of coronary heart disease to cholesterol lowering," *Journal of the American Medical Association* 251 (1984): 351–364, 365–374.

8   "NIH . . . Consensus Panel . . . reported":
     National Institutes of Health Consensus Panel, "Consensus Development Conference Statement," Conference on Lowering Blood Cholesterol (Dec. 10–12, 1984).

9   "Seven Nations Study":
     "Hold the eggs and butter," cover story, *Time* (March 26, 1984): 56–63. A. B. Keys, "Coronary heart disease—The global picture," *Atherosclerosis* 22 (1975): 149–192.

9   "Western Electric . . . studied":
     R. B. Shekelle, A. M. Shyrock, P. Oglesby, et al., "Diet, serum cholesterol, and death from coronary heart disease: The Western Electric Study," *New England Journal of Medicine* 304 (1981): 65.

9   "Framingham Heart Study":
        T. R. Dawber, R. J. Nickerson, et al., "Eggs, serum cholesterol and cor-
        onary heart disease," *American Journal of Clinical Nutrition* 36 (1982):
        617–625.
10   "Dr. William P. Castelli":
        Jane E. Brody, "Heart disease: Big study produces new data, *New York
        Times* (Jan. 8, 1985):C-1, 4.
10   "Early fatalities . . . not exclusively a phenomenon of recent times":
        "Hold the eggs and butter," cover story, *Time* (Mar. 26, 1984):56–63.
11   "Although people have suffered . . . the term 'heart attack'":
        R. A. Kunin, *Mega-Nutrition* (New York: McGraw-Hill, 1980), p. 50.
11   "University of Utah Medical Center":
        P. N. Hopkins and R. R. Williams, "A survey of 246 suggested coronary
        risk factors," *Atherosclerosis* 40 (1981):1–52.
13   "Heart attacks . . . responsible for more deaths":
        NHLBI Lipids Research Clinics Program, "The lipid research clinics cor-
        onary primary prevention trial results. I. Reduction in incidence of coronary
        heart disease. II. The relationship of reduction in incidence of coronary heart
        disease to cholesterol lowering," *Journal of the American Medical Association*
        251 (1984):351–364, 365–374.
15   "AMA has been recommending":
        Nutrition News Briefs 4 (1984).
15   "Since 1963 the average American cholesterol intake":
        R. I. Levy, "Causes of the decline in cardiovascular mortality," in "The
        decline in coronary heart disease mortality—The role of cholesterol change?"
        Proceedings of a symposium held in Anaheim, California, November 13,
        1983, in cooperation with the College of Physicians and Surgeons of Colum-
        bia University. Monograph, Mead Johnson Pharmaceutical Division, pp.
        10–16.
16   "Premenopausal women":
        "Hold the eggs and butter," cover story, *Time* (Mar. 26, 1984) 56–63 and
        J. L. Sullivan, "The sex difference in ischemic heart disease," *Perspectives in
        Biology and Medicine* 26 (1984):657–671.
16   "The Korean War":
        "Hold the eggs and butter," cover story, *Time* (Mar. 26, 1984):56–63.
18   "The liver produces":
        R. P. Cook, *Cholesterol* (New York: Academic Press, 1958), p. 1–2.
19   "A simple fingerprint screening test":
        "Cardiologists balance research into heart ailments with studies on side
        effects of drugs," *Newark Star-Ledger* (Dec. 16, 1984): Sec. 1, p. 97.
19   "laser coronary angioplasty":
        Sandra Blakeslee, "Laser is designed to clean arteries," *New York Times*
        (Jan. 29, 1985): C-1, C-8.

PART ONE, CHAPTER 2. NOT ONLY IN AMERICA

21   "Historically, . . . more common in West . . . than Far East," "In south-
        ern Japan," and "Kirghiz steppe":

A. B. Keys, "Coronary heart disease—The global picture," *Atherosclerosis* 22 (1975): 149–192.

21   "Also, Japanese in Hawaii":
A. B. Keys, "Coronary heart disease—The global picture," *Atherosclerosis* 22 (1975):149–192 and H. Kato, J. Tillotson, et al., "Epidemiologic studies of coronary heart disease and stroke in Japanese men living in Japan, Hawaii, and California: Serum lipids and diet," *American Journal of Epidemiology* 97 (1973):372.

22   "Dr. De Langen":
A. B. Keys, "Coronary heart disease—The global picture," *Atherosclerosis* 22 (1975):149–192.

22   "When Yemenite Jews":
A. B. Keys, "Coronary heart disease—The global picture," *Atherosclerosis* 22 (1975):149–192.

22   "Bantu and Eurafrican patients" and "the Navajo Indians":
A. B. Keys, "Coronary heart disease—The global picture," *Atherosclerosis* 22 (1975):149–192.

23   "Early Eskimo" and "With the exception of the Masai tribe":
A. B. Keys, "Coronary heart disease—The global picture," *Atherosclerosis* 22 (1975):149–192.

23   "The Puerto Rico Heart Health Program":
T. Gordon, A. Kagan, et al., "Diet and its relation to coronary heart disease and death in three populations," *Circulation* 63 (1981):500–514.

24   "Diets in rural Greece":
A. B. Keys, "Coronary heart disease—The global picture," *Atherosclerosis* 22 (1975):149–192.

24   "Very Recent Research":
F. H. Mattson, S. M. Grundy, "Comparison of effect of dietary saturated, monounsaturated, and polyunsaturated fatty acids on plasma lipids and lipoproteins in man," *Journal of Lipid Research* 26 (1985):194–202.

24   "Norway" and "England":
A. B. Keys, "Coronary heart disease—The global picture," *Atherosclerosis* 22 (1975):149–192.

25   "German prisoners of war":
L. E. Lamb, "Diet to prevent heart attacks and strokes," *The Health Letter* 15 (Feb. 22, 1980):1.

25   "In 1981 *Lancet* . . . Oslo men":
I. Hjermann, I. Holme, et al., "Effect of diet and smoking intervention on the incidence of coronary heart disease," Report from the Oslo study of a randomized trial in healthy men, *Lancet* (Dec. 12, 1981):1303–1310.

26   "a study of . . . North Karelia":
C. Ehnholm, J. K. Huttunen, "Effect of diet on serum lipoproteins in a population with a high risk of coronary heart disease," *New England Journal of Medicine* 307 (1982):850–855.

26   "Also in Finland":
M. Miettinen, M. Karvonen, et al., "Effect of cholesterol-lowering diet on mortality from coronary heart disease and other causes: A twelve-year clinical trial in men and women," *Lancet* (Oct. 21, 1972):835–838.

26   "The diet of the Israelis":

A. Palgi, "Association between dietary changes and mortality rates: Israel 1949 to 1977; a trend-free regression model," *American Journal of Clinical Nutrition* 34 (1981):1569–1583.

27   "Over a period . . . older European Jews in Israel":

M. Shadel, "Diet, fatty acids, and atherosclerosis: A study of aged Yemenite and European immigrants to Israel," *Geriatrics* 21 (1966):159–164.

27   "The habitual diets of . . . Pukapuka and Tokelau":

I. A. Prior, F. Davidson, "Cholesterol, coconuts, and diet on Polynesian atolls; a natural experiment: The Pukapuka and Tokelau Island studies," *American Journal of Clinical Nutrition* 34 (1981):1552–1581.

27   "The Maoris":

R. Beaglehole, M. A. Foulkes, et al., "Cholesterol and mortality in New Zealand Maoris," *British Medical Journal* (Feb. 1980):285–294.

28   "The Rarotongans":

J. D. Hunter, "Diet, body build, blood pressure and serum cholesterol levels with coconut-eating Polynesians," *Federation Proceedings* 21 (1962): 36–43.

28   "For example, in Japan":

A. B. Keys, "Coronary heart disease—The global picture," *Atherosclerosis* 22 (1975):149–192.

28   "China, historically":

C. J. Glueck and W. E. Connor, "Diet-coronary heart disease relationship reconnoitered," *American Journal of Clinical Nutrition* 21 (1978):727–737.

PART ONE, CHAPTER 3. THE CHOLESTEROL FAMILY: BAD MEMBERS— AND THE GOOD ONE

30   "What exactly is cholesterol?":

The discussion of cholesterol and lipid biochemistry and metabolism in this chapter is drawn from R. P. Cook, *Cholesterol* (New York: Academic Press, 1958) and P. A. Mayes, "Lipids," "Metabolism of lipids: I. Fatty acids. II. Role of the tissues," and "Regulation of carbohydrate and lipid metabolism," Chapters 16–19 in D. W. Martin, Jr., P. A. Mayes, and V. W. Rodwell, *Harper's Review of Biochemistry*, 19th edition (Los Altos, California: Lange Medical Publications, 1983).

35   "The discovery of cholesterol":

R. P. Cook, *Cholesterol* (New York: Academic Press, 1958), pp. 1–2.

38   "Chicken fat and human milk fat":

W. Insull, Jr., J. Hirsch, T. James, and E. H. Ahrens, Jr., "The fatty acids of human milk: II. Alterations produced by manipulation of caloric balance and exchange of dietary fats," *Journal of Clinical Investigation* 38 (1959): 443–450 and A. S. Feigenbaum and H. Fisher, "The influence of dietary fat on the incorporation of fatty acids into body and egg fat of the hen," *Archives of Biochemistry and Biophysics* 79 (1959):302–306.

38   "As Dr. Henry Blackburn . . . has observed":

Jerry E. Bishop, "Scientists are firming up cholesterol connection with coronary disease," *Wall Street Journal* (Jan. 10, 1984):16.

38   "The Pima Indians of Arizona":
            "Hold the eggs and butter," cover story, *Time* (Mar. 26, 1984):56–63
and A. B. Keys, "Coronary heart disease—The global picture," *Atherosclerosis* 22 (1975):149–192.
39   "The Masai, a nomadic tribe of East Africa" and "the camel-herding
            Rendille":
            A. Keys, "Coronary heart disease—The global picture," *Atherosclerosis*
22 (1975):149–192.
39   "Maybe no more than one or two percent of Americans":
            "Hold the eggs and butter," cover story, *Time* (Mar. 26, 1984):56–63.
40   "If that ratio is less than 1 part HDL to 4.5 parts":
            Jane E. Brody, "Heart disease: Big study produces new data," *New York
Times* (Jan. 8, 1985): C-1.

PART ONE, CHAPTER 4. CHOLESTEROL: THE DIMINISHING
CONTROVERSY

42   "Since 1980 . . . have been publishing a brochure":
            "Hold the eggs and butter," cover story, *Time* (Mar. 26, 1984):56–63.
42   "The Council on Scientific Affairs of the AMA":
            Council on Scientific Affairs, "Dietary and pharmacologic therapy for
the lipid risk factors," *Journal of the American Medical Association* 250
(1983):1873–1879.
43   "In short, . . . bury 'with full military honors'":
            B. A. Barnes and C. W. Barnes, *Solved: The Riddle of Heart Attacks*
(Fort Collins, Colorado: Robinson Press, 1976), p. 67.
43   "Thus, it is claimed, the actual number of heart attacks":
            B. A. Barnes and C. W. Barnes, *Solved: The Riddle of Heart Attacks*
(Fort Collins, Colorado: Robinson Press, 1976), pp. 7–12.
44   "In June 1983, *Nutrition Today*":
            "Nutrition's own Mount Saint Helens," editorial, *Nutrition Today* (May/
June 1980):6.
44   "The two documents were *Toward Healthful Diets* and the Hulley
            Report":
            Food and Nutrition Board of the National Research Council, *Toward
Healthful Diets* (National Academy of Sciences, 1980), also in *Nutrition Today* (May/June 1980):7–11, and S. B. Hulley, R. M. Rosenman, R. D.
Bawol, and R. J. Brand, "Epidemiology as a guide to clinical decisions," *New
England Journal of Medicine* (1980), reprinted in *Nutrition Today* (May/June
1980):21–26.
45   "opined Milton L. Scott":
            B. C. Breidenstein, *Exploring the Known* (pamphlet published by the
National Livestock and Meat Board, 1983).
45   "inquired Robert M. Kark, M.D.":
            B. C. Breidenstein, *Exploring the Known* (pamphlet published by the
National Livestock and Meat Board, 1983).

46   "obesity is a killer":
        G. Kolata, "Obesity declared a disease," *Science* 227 (1985): 1019–1021.
46   "wrote Dr. George V. Mann":
        G. V. Mann, "Cholesterol: End of an era," *New England Journal of Medicine* 297 (1977): 644–650.
46   "Research and Nutrition Information of the National Live Stock and Meat Board" and "speaking at an American Feed Manufacturers Association": W. Anderson, "Feed industry challenged to join other groups in clarifying diet-health issue," *Feedstuffs* (May 28, 1984): 1.
47   "breakdown of such fats . . . might be toxic":
        B. O. Barnes and C. W. Barnes, *Solved: The Riddle of Heart Attacks* (Fort Collins, Colorado: Robinson Press, 1976), p. 73.
48   "The periodical *Feedstuffs* charged":
        "Cholesterol 'interpretations' continue to mislead," *Feedstuffs* (Feb. 20, 1984): 8.
48   "The drug cholestyramine . . . *Nutrition Today* remarked":
        C. F. Enloe, "Coronary disease prevention should be individualized," editorial in *Nutrition Today* 19 (1984): 12–14 and "Diet and heart disease: Responses to the LRC-CPPT findings," *Nutrition Today* 19 (1984): 20–26, 20 (1984): 20–25.
48   "*Science* took the study to task":
        G. Kolata, "Heart panel's conclusions questioned," *Science* 227 (1985): 40–41.
48   "Dr. Richard A. Kunin":
        R. A. Kunin, *Mega-Nutrition* (New York: McGraw-Hill, 1980), p. 55.
49   " 'I have a strong impression,' writes Dr. Roger J. Williams:
        R. A. Kunin, *Mega-Nutrition* (New York: McGraw-Hill, 1980), p. 59.
49   "declares Dr. Carl Pfeiffer":
        R. A. Kunin, *Mega-Nutrition* (New York: McGraw-Hill, 1980), p. 68.
49   "There are those advocates of . . . massive amounts of Vitamin C":
        R. A. Kunin, *Mega-Nutrition* (New York: McGraw-Hill, 1980), p. 71.
50   " 'Cholesterol levels of most people' ":
        "Cholesterol levels of most people not affected by food eaten, Missouri study shows," *Poultry Times* (Aug. 12, 1984) and M. Flynn, A. Anderson, et al., "Eggs, serum lipids, emotional stress, and blood pressure in medical students," *Archives of Environmental Health* 29 (1984): 90.
51   "*Science* reported the observations of Dr. Daniel Steinberg":
        D. Steinberg, letter to editor, *Science* 227 (1985): 582 and C. Lenfant, B. Rifkind, and I. Jacoby, letter to editor, same issue, 583–584.

PART TWO, CHAPTER 1. HOW CHOLESTEROL-CONSCIOUS ARE WE . . . REALLY?

57   "but according to the Department of Agriculture":
        "Household food consumption survey 1965–66," Report No. 1, U.S. Department of Agriculture, Agricultural Research Service and E. M. Pao, K. H. Fleming, P. M. Guenther, and S. J. Mickle, "Foods commonly eaten by individuals: Amount per day and per eating occasion," U.S. Department of Agricul-

ture, Human Nutrition Information Service, Home Economic Research Report No. 44, 1982.

57   "Restaurateurs catering to affluent"
      Marian Burros, "Responding to the call to cut fats, cholesterol," *New York Times* (Jan. 23, 1985): C-4.

PART TWO, CHAPTER 2. DIETARY FRIENDS AND ENEMIES

60   "Similarly, when groups . . . who habitually consumed at least one egg a day":
      A. C. Beynen and M. B. Katan, letter to editor, *Nutrition Reviews* 42 (1984): 201.

60   "The Framingham Study, in its earlier phases":
      T. R. Dawber, R. J. Nickerson, et al., "Eggs, serum cholesterol and coronary heart disease," *American Journal of Clinical Nutrition* 36 (1982): 617–625.

60   "As *Nutrition Reviews* observed":
      "The influence of eggs upon plasma cholesterol levels," *Nutrition Reviews* 41 (1983): 272–274 and H. Fisher and G. A. Leveille, "Observations on the cholesterol, linoleic and linolenic acid content of eggs as influenced by dietary fats," *Journal of Nutrition* 63 (1957): 119–129.

61   "The Cleveland Clinic Foundation . . . study . . . to compare . . . ordinary and modified eggs":
      H. B. Brown and H. Page, "Effect of polyunsaturated eggs on serum cholesterol," *Journal of the American Dietetic Association* 46 (1965): 189–192.

62   "This particular conclusion goes contrary":
      E. C. Naber, "The cholesterol problem, the egg and lipid metabolism in the laying hen," *Poultry Science* 55 (1976): 14–30.

62   "In experiments with animals, eggs prepared in different ways":
      O. J. Pollak, "Serum cholesterol levels resulting from various egg diets—Experimental studies with clinical implications," *Journal of the American Geriatric Association* 6 (1958): 614.

63   "sources of possibly harmful derivatives":
      C. B. Taylor, S-K. Peng, et al., "Spontaneously occurring angiotoxic derivatives of cholesterol," *American Journal of Clinical Nutrition* 32 (1979): 40–57.

64   "In experiments with daily cholesterol supplements":
      A. Keys and R. W. Parlin, "Serum cholesterol response to changes in dietary lipids," *American Journal of Clinical Nutrition* 19 (1966): 175–181.

64   "Harvard researchers found":
      D. M. Hegsted, R. B. McGandy, M. L. Myers, and F. J. Stare, "Quantitative effects of dietary fat on serum cholesterol in man," *American Journal of Clinical Nutrition* 17 (1965): 281–295.

65

      "Whether or not they are labeled essential, linolenic acid . . . found to lower blood cholesterol about 170 times more":
      D. F. Horrobin and M. S. Manku, "How do fatty acids lower plasma cholesterol levels?" *Lipids* 18 (1983): 558–562.

66   "Even relatively small changes in the polyunsaturated/saturated . . . ratio":
R. L. Jackson, M. L. Kashyap, R. L. Barnhart, et al., "Influence of poly-unsaturated and saturated fats on plasma lipids and lipoproteins in man," *American Journal of Clinical Nutrition* 39 (1984):589–597.

66   "The *Journal of Human Nutrition* reported":
S. Furniss, "The effect of a strict polyunsaturated fat (PUF) diet on the serum lipids of normolipidemic subjects," *Journal of Human Nutrition* 31 (1977):377–379.

66   "*Lancet* cited an average 22-percent drop":
E. H. Ahrens, Jr., J. Hirsch, W. Insoll, Jr., R. Blomstrand, and M. L. Pe-terson, "The influence of dietary fats on serum-lipid levels in man," *Lancet* (May 11, 1957):943–953.

66   "When the Finnish subjects were placed":
J. M. Iacono, P. Puska, R. M. Dougherty, et al., "Effect of dietary fat on blood pressure in a rural Finnish population," *American Journal of Clinical Nutrition* 38 (1983):860–869.

67   "The only essential difference was that one group was vegetarian":
M. Liebman and T. L. Bazzarre, "Plasma lipids of vegetarian and non-vegetarian males: Effects of egg consumption," *American Journal of Clinical Nutrition* 38 (1983):612–619.

67   "Food fiber has long been recognized":
A good, nontechnical introduction to research on dietary fiber is L. Gal-ton, *The Truth about Fiber in Your Food* (New York: Crown, 1976).

68   "To the nutritionist, dietary fiber is":
H. Trowell, "The development of the concept of dietary fiber in human nutrition," *American Journal of Clinical Nutrition* 25 (1978):S3–S11.

68   "Pectin, for instance, interacts helpfully":
M. M. Baig and J. J. Cerda, "Pectin: Its interaction with serum lipopro-teins," *American Journal of Clinical Nutrition* 34 (1981):50–53.

68   "When University of Minnesota researchers":
L. Vaughn, "Getting the most out of the F-complex," *Prevention* (Sept. 1984):50–52.

68   "For example, a statistically significant retardation of spontaneous atherogenesis":
H. Fisher, P. Griminger, and H. S. Weiss, "Avian atherosclerosis: retarda-tion by pectin," *Science* 146 (1964):1063–1064.

69   "Our own discovery of the powers of pectin":
H. Fisher, H. S. Weiss, and P. Griminger, "Effect of prolonged dietary treatment on atherosclerosis in the mature fowl," *Journal of Atherosclerosis Research* 3 (1963):57–67.

69   "Then, in human volunteers, we found":
H. Fisher, P. Griminger, E. R. Sostman, et al., "Dietary pectin and blood cholesterol," *Journal of Nutrition* 86 (1965):113.

69   "The main function in the body of dietary lignin":
J. L. Kelsay, "A review of research on effects of fiber intake in man," *American Journal of Clinical Nutrition* 31 (1978):102–119.

70   "Scientists have found various gums":
D. Kritchevsky, "Dietary fiber: What it is and what it does," in *Food and*

Nutrition in Health and Disease (New York: Annals of the New York Academy of Sciences, Vol. 300, 1977):283–289.

71   "In a study reported in the *American Journal of Clinical Nutrition*":
G. Fraser, D. R. Jacobs, et al., "The effect of various vegetable supplements on serum cholesterol," *American Journal of Clinical Nutrition* 34 (1981):1272–1277.

71   "One of the most impressive research findings comes out of India:"
F. Grande, J. T. Anderson, and A. Keys, "Effect of carbohydrates of leguminous seeds, wheat and potatoes on serum cholesterol concentrations in man," *American Journal of Clinical Nutrition* 86 (1965):313–317.

71   "In the Netherlands, Trappist monks":
J. J. Groen, K. B. Tijong, et al., "The influence of nutrition and ways of life on blood cholesterol and the prevalence of hypertension and coronary heart disease among trappist and benedictine Monks," *American Journal of Clinical Nutrition* 10 (1962):456–470 and J. J. Groen, "Why bread in the diet lowers serum cholesterol," *Proceedings of the Nutrition Society* 32 (1973): 159–167.

71   "Dr. James W. Anderson, of the University of Kentucky":
L. Vaughn, "Getting the most out of the F-complex," *Prevention* (Sept. 1984):52.

72   "A decade or so ago the Senate Committee on Dietary Goals":
U.S. Senate Select Committee on Nutrition and Human Needs, "Dietary goals for the United States," second edition (Washington, D.C.: U.S. Government Printing Office, 1977).

72   "The Nazis believed that white bread":
E. J. Kahn, Jr., "The staffs of life: II. Man is what he eats," *The New Yorker* (Nov. 12, 1984):56.

73   "Trappist monks, Arab bedouins, and Yemenite Jews":
J. J. Groen, "Why bread in the diet lowers serum cholesterol," *Proceedings of the Nutrition Society* 32 (1973):159–167.

73   "the Food and Agriculture Organization of the United Nations has noted":
E. J. Kahn, Jr., "The staffs of life: II. Man is what he eats," *The New Yorker* (Nov. 12, 1984):58.

73   "Certain groups of South African blacks":
H. Trowell, "The development of the concept of dietary fiber in human nutrition," *American Journal of Clinical Nutrition* 25 (1978):S3–S11.

73   "In a University of Alberta study":
G. D. Brown, L. Whyte, et al., "Effects of two 'lipid lowering' diets on plasma lipid levels of patients with peripheral vascular disease," *Journal of the American Dietetic Association* 84 (1984):546–550.

74   "Sweet potatoes score highest":
E. D. Lund, "Cholesterol binding capacity of fiber from tropical fruits and vegetables," *Lipids* 19 (1983):85–90.

74   "How much fiber should we include":
L. Galton, *The Truth about Fiber in Your Food*, (New York: Crown, 1976), pp. 128–129.

74   "Since the time of Hippocrates" and "It may also improve carbohydrate (sugar) tolerance":

H. Trowell, "The development of the concept of dietary fiber in human nutrition," *American Journal of Clinical Nutrition* 25 (1978): S3–S11.

75   " 'LDL cholesterol can be reduced . . . by consuming a cup of oat bran a day' ":
"Hold the eggs and butter," cover story, *Time* (Mar. 26, 1984): 56–63 and R. W. Kirby, J. W. Anderson, et al., "Oat-bran selectively lowers serum low-density lipoprotein cholesterol concentrations of hypercholesterolemic men," *American Journal of Clinical Nutrition* 34 (1981): 824–829.

75   "The blood cholesterol-lowering effect of whole ground oats":
H. Fisher, P. Griminger, "Cholesterol-lowering effects of certain grains and of oat fractions in the chick," *Proceedings of the Society for Experimental Biology and Medicine* 126 (1967): 108–111.

75   "Garlic's credentials are formidable and rooted in history":
Jane E. Brody, "Personal Health," column in *New York Times* (Oct. 3, 1984): C-10.

76   "Under the supervision of Tagore Medical College":
A. Bordia, "Effect of garlic on blood lipids in patients with coronary heart disease," *American Journal of Clinical Nutrition* 34 (1981): 2100–2103.

76   "Other researchers have found that garlic oil can inhibit clot formation":
R. C. Jain and D. B. Konar, "Effect of garlic oil in experimental cholesterol atherosclerosis," *Atherosclerosis* 29 (1978): 125–129.

76   "Research reported in the journal *Atherosclerosis*":
A. Bordia, H. S. Bansal, et al., "Effect of the essential oils of garlic and onion on alimentary hyperlipemia," *Atherosclerosis* 21 (1975): 15–19.

76   "among chicks fed cholesterol and saponins":
P. Griminger and H. Fisher, "Dietary saponin and plasma cholesterol in the chicken," *Proceedings of the Society for Experimental Biology and Medicine* 99 (1958): 424–426.

77   "The shiitake, or Japanese forest mushroom":
S. Suzuki and S. Ohshima, "Influence of shii-ta-ke (*Lentinus edodes*) on human serum cholesterol," *Mushroom Science* 9 (1974): 463–467.

77   "Eritadenine, a derivative":
K. Takashima and K. Izumi, "The hypocholesterolemic action of eritadenine in the rat," *Atherosclerosis* 17 (1973): 491–502.

77   "Avocados":
W. C. Grant, "Influence of avocados on serum cholesterol," *Federation Proceedings* 19 (1960): 18.

78   "scientists have determined . . . a delay of 24 to 72 hours before cholesterol in food":
E. Karvinen, T. M. Lin, et al., "Capacity of the human intestine to absorb exogenous cholesterol," *Journal of Applied Physiology* 2 (1957): 143–147.

78   "Cholesterol is absorbed in three stages":
R. Booth and J. Glover, "Inhibition of cholesterol absorption by 'foreign' sterol," *Biochemical Journal* 103 (1967): 29.

78   "Cholesterol absorption decreases when plant sterols are added":
F. H. Mattson, R. A. Volpenheim, et al., "Effect of plant sterol esters on absorption of dietary cholesterol," *Journal of Nutrition* 107 (1977): 1139–1146.

79   "The Seventh Day Adventists had significantly lower levels":
        L. A. Simons, J. C. Gibson, "The influence of a wide range of absorbed
cholesterol on plasma cholesterol levels in man," *American Journal of Clinical
Nutrition* 31 (1978): 1334–1339.

79   "In another study, university students":
        J. M. R. Beveridge, H. L. Haust, and W. F. Connell, "Magnitude of the
hypocholesterolemic effect of dietary sitosterol in man," *Journal of Nutrition*
83 (1964): 119–122.

79   "In still another study, reported in the *Canadian Journal of Biochemistry
and Physiology*":
        J. M. R. Beveridge, W. F. Connell, and G. A. Mayer, "The nature of the
substances in dietary fat affecting the level of plasma cholesterol in humans,"
Canadian Journal of Biochemistry and Physiology 35 (1957): 257–270.

79   "There is evidence that sterols from the sea":
        E. Reiner, J. Topliff, and J. D. Wood, "Hypocholesterolemic agents de-
rived from sterols of marine algae," *Canadian Journal of Biochemistry and
Physiology* 40 (1962): 1401–1406.

79   "Collectively, these protective substances":
        Jane E. Brody, "Fish is good for the heart," *New York Times* (Jun. 13,
1984): C-1, 12.

79-80   "reduced both the quantity and adhesiveness of clot-forming platelets":
        T. A. B. Sanders and M. C. Hochland, "A comparison of the influence on
plasma lipids and platelet function of supplements of omega-3 and omega-6
polyunsaturated fatty acids," *British Journal of Nutrition* 50 (1983): 521–529.

80   "Eskimos living in Point Hope":
        L.-J. Ho, B. Mikkelson, et al., "Alaskan Arctic Eskimo: Responses to a
customary high-fat diet," guest editorial, *American Journal of Clinical Nutrition* 25 (1972) 737–745.

80   "an observer reported in *Lancet*":
        J. Dyerberg, H. O. Bang, and E. Stofferson," Eicosapentaenoic acid
and prevention of thrombosis and atherosclerosis," *Lancet* (Jul. 15, 1978):
117–119.

80   "*Nutrition Reviews* has pointed out":
        "Marine oils and platelet function in man," *Nutrition Reviews* 42 (1984):
189–191.

80   "Eating fish or fish oils may offer protection":
        D. Kromhout, E. B. Bosschieter, C. De Lezenne Coulaoder, "The in-
verse relation between fish consumption and twenty-year mortality from coronary heart disease," *New England Journal of Medicine* 312 (1985): 1205–
1209 and B. E. Phillipson, D. W. Rothrock, W. E. Connor, W. S. Harris, D. R.
Illingworth, "Reduction of plasma lipids, lipoproteins, and apoproteins by dietary fish oils in patients with hypertriglyceridemia, *New England Journal of
Medicine* 312 (1985): 1210–1216.

81   "Among the 'fatty' fishes coming back into favor":
        Jane E. Brody, "Fish is good for the heart," *New York Times* (Jun. 13,
1984): C-1, 12.

82   "a study described in *Atherosclerosis* in 1983":
        P. Singer, W. Jaeger, et al., "Lipid and blood pressure-lowering effect of
mackerel diet in man," *Atherosclerosis* 49 (1983): 99–108.

82   "cautioned Dr. William E. Connor":
          Jane E. Brody, "Fish is good for the heart," *New York Times* (Jun. 13, 1984):C-1, 12.

83   "Although many claims are made for . . . vitamin C":
          V. E. Peterson, P. A. Crapo, et al., "Quantification of plasma cholesterol and triglyceride levels in hypercholesterolemic subjects receiving ascorbic acid supplements," *American Journal of Clinical Nutrition* 28 (1975):584–587 and Nutrition Reviews, *Present Knowledge in Nutrition*, fifth edition (Washington D.C.: The Nutrition Foundation, 1984), Chapter 18, p. 265.

83   "Vitamin E, administered in amounts":
          J. P. Nitikin, "Effect of vitamin E on blood lipids and coagulability in patients with atherosclerosis," abstract, *Nutrition Abstracts and Reviews* 33 (1963):519.

83   "Supplements of calcium carbonate":
          M. L. Bierenbaum, A. I. Fleischman, and R. I. Raichelson, "Long term human studies on the lipid effects of oral calcium," *Lipids* 7 (1972):202–206.

83   "In a study reported in the *American Journal of Clinical Nutrition*":
          A. K. Bhattacharyya, C. Thera, et al., "Dietary calcium and fat," *American Journal of Clinical Nutrition* 22 (1969):1161–1174.

83   "The softer the drinking water, the higher the cardiovascular death rate":
          M. D. Crawford, "Hardness of drinking water and cardiovascular disease," *Proceedings of the Nutrition Society* 31 (1972):347.

84   "Other evidence for the effect of water":
          H. A. Schroeder, "Relation between mortality from cardiovascular disease and treated water supplies," *Journal of the American Medical Association* 172 (1960):1902–1908.

84   "The difference between hard and soft drinking water can amount to 200 mg of calcium":
          M. D. Crawford, "Hardness of drinking water and cardiovascular disease," *Proceedings of the Nutrition Society* 31 (1972):347.

84   "The average American consumes 120 pounds of sugar":
          Jane E. Brody, "Personal Health," *New York Times* (Mar. 13, 1985):C-6.

85   "Sugar was once placed alongside saturated fat and cholesterol":
          J. Yudkin and J. Morland, "Sugar intake and myocardial infarction," *American Journal of Clinical Nutrition* 20 (1967):503–506.

85   "However, many clinical observations":
          A. Keys, "Coronary heart disease—The global picture," *Atherosclerosis* 22 (1975):149–192.

85   "cholesterol drops if sugar . . . is replaced with leafy vegetables":
          F. Grande, J. T. Auderson, and A. Keys, "Sucrose and various carbohydrate-containing foods and serum lipids in man," *American Journal of Clinical Nutrition* 27 (1974):1043–1051.

85   "observed that . . . subjects complained of hunger":
          R. E. Hodges and W. H. Krehl, "The role of carbohydrates in lipid metabolism," *American Journal of Clinical Nutrition* 17 (1965):334–346.

86   "Milk apparently contains a cholesterol-lowering factor":
          A. N. Howard and J. Marks, "Hypocholesterolemic effect of milk," *Lancet* (1977):225–256.

86   "Nevertheless, when a group of Masai men":

G. V. Mann and A. Spoerry, "Studies of a surfactant and cholesterolemia in the Masai," *American Journal of Clinical Nutrition* 27 (1974):464–469.

86   "There is some evidence that, in children and young adults, the rate of liver synthesis":

B. J. Dull, R. D. McCarthy, and A. Kilara," The modulating effect of an inhibitor of cholesterolgenesis present in bovine milk upon the synthesis of cholesterol, dolichol and ubiquinone," *Atherosclerosis* 49 (1983):231–239.

86

"Skim milk, in a test with adolescent schoolboys":

J. Rossouw, E.-M. Burger, et al. "The effect of skim milk, yoghurt, and full cream milk on human serum lipids," *American Journal of Clinical Nutrition* 34 (1981):351–356.

87   "One study gave different groups of healthy young volunteers":

L. U. Thompson, D. J. A. Jenkins, et al., "The effect of fermented and non-fermented milks on serum cholesterol," *American Journal of Clinical Nutrition* 27 (1974):464–469.

87   "Yogurt and calcium supplements were used":

T. L. Bazzarre, S. LiuWu, J. A. Kuhas, "Total and HDL-cholesterol concentrations following yogurt and calcium supplementation," *Nutrition Reports International* 28 (1983):1225–1232.

87   "A study from Norway, reported in *The New England Journal of Medicine*":

H. Jick, O. S. Miettinen, et al., "Coffee and myocardial infarction," *New England Journal of Medicine*: 289 (1973):63–67 and P. Williams, P. Wood, and J. Albers, "Coffee intake and elevated cholesterol and apolipoprotein B levels in men," *Journal of the American Medical Association* 253 (1985): 1407–1411.

88   "For example, the prestigious *Harvard Medical School Health Letter*":

"Moderation versus abuse: Or, how much alcohol is safe?" *Harvard Medical School Health Letter* 7 (Dec. 1981):1.

88   "A study conducted at King's College in London":

C. G. Fenn and J. M. Littleton, "Interactions between ethanol and dietary fat in determining human platelet function," *Thrombosis and Haemostasis* 51 (1984):50–53.

89   "Alcohol has been shown to raise blood HDL levels"

"Changes in plasma lipoproteins due to alcohol consumption," *Nutrition Reviews* 43 (1985):74–76.

PART TWO, CHAPTER 3. EXERCISE: THE SECOND BEST REGULATOR

90   "More are like James Michener":

James Michener, "An ailing heart," *New York Times Sunday Magazine* (Aug. 19, 1984):26.

91   "The important Framingham Study" and "communal settlements in Israel":

A. Keys, "Coronary heart disease—The Global picture," *Atherosclerosis* 22 (1975):149–192.

91   "Also, in London, postal clerks," "a report on District of Columbia postal workers," and "London bus drivers":

A. Keys, "Coronary heart disease—The global picture," *Atherosclerosis* 22 (1975): 149–192.

92   "However, a study of a Swiss Alpine population":

D. Gsell and J. Mayer, "Low blood cholesterol associated with high calorie, high saturated fat intakes in a Swiss Alpine village population," *American Journal of Clinical Nutrition* 10 (1962): 471–474.

92   "An occupational analysis . . . of 226 Caucasian men":

A. Keys, "Coronary heart disease—The global picture," *Atherosclerosis* 22 (1975): 149–192.

93   "A case in point is the 1974 monograph":

A. Keys, "Coronary heart disease—The global picture," *Atherosclerosis* 22 (1975): 149–192.

93   "In another British study . . . 15,171 men":

N. Hickey, R. Mulcahy, et al., "Study of coronary risk factors related to physical activity in 15,171 men," *British Medical Journal* (Aug. 30, 1975): 507–509.

93   "Comparisons between geographically separated brothers":

M. F. Trulson, R. E. Clancy, et al., "Comparisons of siblings in Boston and Ireland," *Journal of the American Dietetic Association* 45 (1964): 225 and J. Brown, G. J. Bourke, et al., "Nutritional and epidemiologic factors related to heart disease," *World Review of Nutrition and Dietetics* 12 (1970): 1–41.

94   "Observations of men ski-racing in Sweden":

L. A. Carlson and F. Mossfeldt, "Acute effects of prolonged, heavy exercise on the concentration of plasma lipids and lipoproteins in man," *Acta Physiologica Scandinavica* (1964): 51–59.

94   "Under the auspices of the Netherlands Institute of Nutrition":

L. M. Dalderup, N. de Voogd, et al., "The effects of increasing the daily physical activity on the serum cholesterol levels," *Nutritio et Dieta* 9 (1967): 112–123.

94   "One such experiment focussed . . . on treadmill running":

D. E. Campbell, "Influence of diet and physical activity on blood serum cholesterol of young men," *American Journal of Clinical Nutrition* 18 (1966): 79–85.

94   "In another study . . . 133 young men":

D. E. Campbell, "Influence of several physical activities on serum cholesterol concentrations in young men," *Journal of Lipid Research* 6 (1965): 478–480.

95   "notes Dr. Larry Gibbons":

"Which fights cholesterol best?" *Prevention* (Jan. 1985): 90.

96   "The foremost American proponent of running, Mr. Fixx dropped dead of a heart attack at 52":

James Michener, "An ailing heart," *New York Times Sunday Magazine* (Aug. 19, 1984): 26.

96   "For example, thirteen members of the Australian National University Mountaineering Club":

P. J. Nestel, M. Podolinski, and N. H. Fidge, "Marked increase in high density lipoproteins in mountaineers," *Atherosclerosis* 34 (1979): 143–146.

96   "Also, the Laboratory of Physiological Hygiene":

G. Sopko and D. R. Jacobs, Jr., "Effects on blood lipids and body weight in high risk men of a practical exercise program," *Atherosclerosis* 49 (1983): 219–229.

97   "Finnish researchers, too, investigated the effects of moderate physical exercise":

J. K. Huttunen, E. Lansimies, et al., "Effect of moderate physical exercise on serum lipoproteins," *Circulation* 60 (1979):1220–1229.

PART TWO, CHAPTER 4. UNDER STRESS AND OVERWEIGHT

99   "The personality category known as 'Type A'":

M. Friedman and D. Ulmer, *Treating Type A Behavior—And Your Heart* (New York: Knopf, 1984).

100   "For example, more than 800 men":

Jane E. Brody, "Modifying 'Type A' behavior reduces heart attacks," *New York Times* (Aug. 7, 1984):C-1.

100   "This was one conclusion of the Framingham Heart Study in a follow-up report":

H. B. Hubert et al., "Obesity as an independent risk factor for cardiovascular disease: A 26-year follow-up of participants in the Framingham Heart Study," *Circulation* 67 (1983):965–977.

100   "The Zutphen Study":

D. Kromhout, "Body weight, diet, and serum cholesterol in 87 middle-aged men during ten years of follow-up (The Zutphen Study)," *American Journal of Clinical Nutrition* 38 (1983):591–598.

101   "In a Tecumseh, Michigan, study":

A. B. Nichols, C. Ravenscroft, et al., "Independence of serum lipid levels and dietary habits, the Tecumseh Study," *Journal of the American Medical Association* 236 (1976):1948–1953.

101   "In the Framingham Study as well":

H. B. Hubert, et al., "Obesity as an independent risk factor for cardiovascular disease: A 26-year follow-up of participants in the Framingham Heart Study," *Circulation* 67 (1983):965–977 and A. P. Simopoulos, "The health implications of overweight and obesity," *Nutrition Reviews* 43 (1985): 33–40.

101   "The American Cancer Society and the Metropolitan Life Insurance Company":

A. Keys, "Overweight, obesity, coronary heart disease, and mortality," *Nutrition Reviews* 38 (1980):297–307.

102   "a five- to six-year study of 19,409 Belgian men":

L. E. Lamb, ed., *The Health Letter*, XXII (Aug. 12, 1983), San Antonio, Texas.

PART TWO, CHAPTER 5. AN EARLY START—THAT PROVERBIAL OUNCE OF PREVENTION

103   "Preventive measures can hardly get under way too soon":

G. A. Gresham, "Atherosclerosis: Its origins and development in man," in *Arterial Pollution—An Integrated View on Atherosclerosis*, ed. H. Peeters, G. A. Gresham, and R. Paoletti (New York: Plenum Press, 1983), vol. 58, pp. 7–21.

103   "autopsies of American war casualties in both Vietnam":
J. MacNamara, M. Malot, et al., "Coronary artery disease in combat casualties in Vietnam," *Journal of the American Medical Association* 216 (1971):1185.

104   "Children who will become 'high risk' ":
National Institutes of Health Consensus Panel, "Consensus Development Conference Statement," Conference on Lowering Blood Cholesterol (December 10–12, 1984).

104   "in the opinion of Dr. Carlos A. Dujovne:
Medical & Pharmaceutical Information Bureau, Inc. (Jan. 31, 1985).

104   "And the NIH Consensus Development Panel recommended":
National Institutes of Health Consensus Panel, "Consensus Development Conference Statement," Conference on Lowering Blood Cholesterol (Dec. 10–12, 1984).

104   "detected at birth in umbilical cord blood":
J. I. Mann, "Familial hypercholesterolaemia: Renewed interest in an old problem," *British Medical Journal* 289 (Aug. 18, 1984):396.

104   "Investigations in the Netherlands . . . indicated . . . 30 percent of preschool children":
A. Keys, "Coronary heart disease—The global picture, *Atherosclerosis* 22 (1975):149–192.

104   "But experiments with families":
L. M. Dalderup, R. Doornbos, et al., "A practical method for decreasing the serum cholesterol level in man," *American Journal of Clinical Nutrition* 22 (1969):1521–1530.

105   "In another example, Australian teenagers on vegetarian diets":
C. J. Glueck and W. E. Connor, "Diet-coronary heart disease relationships reconnoitered," *American Journal of Clinical Nutrition* 21 (1978): 727–737.

105   "For example, the 1985 edition of Dr. Spock's *Baby and Child Care*":
Dr. Benjamin Spock and Dr. Michael Rothenberg, *Baby and Child Care*, Fortieth Anniversary edition (New York: Pocket Books, 1985), 328.

105   "And in Scottsdale, Arizona, a private clinic" and "Called 'Feelin' Good' ":
Susan Zarrow, "Do your kids feel *this* good?" *Prevention* (Oct. 1984): 55–58.

105   "Bogalusa Heart Study":
Susan Zarrow, "Do your kids feel *this* good?" *Prevention* (Oct. 1984): 55–58.

106   "Derek Bok, President of Harvard University":
Derek Bok, "Needed: A new way to train doctors," *Harvard Magazine* (May/June 1984):32–43, 70–71.

PART TWO, CHAPTER 6. WOMEN—THE (RELATIVELY) IMMUNE GENDER

107   "The answer is simply that women of child-bearing age":
        J. L. Sullivan, "The sex difference in ischemic heart disease," *Perspectives in Biology and Medicine* 26 (Summer, 1983):657–671 and H. S. Weiss and H. Fisher, "Evaluation of sex and segment differences in spontaneous avian aortic atherosclerosis," *American Journal of Physiology* 197 (1959): 1219–1229.

107   "Women using . . . pills were compared with women who used no oral contraceptives":
        "The pill and heart attacks: New evidence," *Harvard Medical School Health Letter* 7 (Dec. 1981):5.

108   "It has also been suggested that menstruation":
        S. Seely, "Possible reasons for the comparatively high resistance of women to heart disease," *American Heart Journal* 91 (1976):275–280.

PART TWO, CHAPTER 7. OFTENER, SLOWER—AND LESS—IS BETTER

110   "a study of more than 1000 . . . men, described in *Lancet*":
        P. Fabry, J. Fodor, et al., "Meal frequency and ischaemic heart disease," *Lancet* (Jul. 27, 1968):190–191.

111   "a study of 30–50-year-old English engine-drivers":
        P. Fabry, J. Fodor, et al., "The frequency of meals, its relation to overweight, hypercholesterolaemia, and increased glucose tolerance," *Lancet* (Sep. 19, 1964):614–615.

111   "Chickens and other animals show similar characteristics":
        P. Griminger, H. Fisher, et al., "Food restriction and spontaneous avian atherosclerosis," *Life Sciences* 6 (1963):410–414.

111   "Marcia Seligson . . . in *Esquire*":
        Marcia Seligson, "The Esquire nutrition plan," *Esquire* (May 1984):146.

PART TWO, CHAPTER 8. AGING

112   "But the long-term NHLBI heart study has been criticized":
        G. Kolata, "Heart panel's conclusions questioned," *Science* 227 (1985): 40–41.

113   "Miriam Osborne Memorial Home":
        A. A. Albanese, M. L. Woodhull, et al., "Effect of diet on blood cholesterol of the elderly," *Geriatrics* 22 (1967):133–144.

PART TWO, CHAPTER 9. MEDICATION AND SURGERY: LAST RESORTS

114   "The panel convened in December 1984 by the NIH":
        National Institutes of Health Consensus Panel, "Consensus Development Conference Statement," Conference on Lowering Blood Cholesterol (Dec.

10–12, 1984) and "Hold the eggs and butter," cover story, *Time* (Mar. 26, 1984):56–63.

116   "Nicotinic acid decreases the synthesis of LDL":
"Treatment of hyperlipidemia in adults: A joint statement of the Nutrition Committee and the Council on Arteriosclerosis," American Heart Association Special Report *Circulation* 69 (1984):1065A–1090A.

116   "Probucol reduces total cholesterol and LDL":
A. M. Gotto, E. L. Berman, et al., "Recommendations for treatment of hyperlipidemia in adults: A joint statement of the Nutrition Committee and the Council on Arteriosclerosis," American Heart Association Special Report, *Circulation* 69 (1984):1065A–1090A.

116   "probucol seems to change the LDL structure":
Narvszewicz, "A novel mechanism by which probucol lowers low density lipoprotein levels demonstrated in the LDL receptor-deficient rabbit," *Journal of Lipid Research* 25 (1984):1206–1213.

116   "Clofibrate blocks the breakdown of fatty tissue":
A. M. Gotto, E. L. Berman, et al., "Recommendations for treatment of hyperlipidemia in adults: A joint statement of the Nutrition Committee and the Council on Arteriosclerosis," American Heart Association Special Report, *Circulation* 69 (1984) 1065A–1090A.

116   "Various hormones play an important role":
G. S. Kurland, A. S. Freedburg, "Hormones, cholesterol, and coronary atherosclerosis," *Circulation* 22 (1960):464–473.

116   "Thyroid hormones L-thyroxine and D-thyroxine":
"The reduction of serum lipoprotein and cholesterol by L-thyroxine," *Nutrition Reviews* 17 (1959):303–304 and C. Dufault, G. Trembley, et al., "Influence of dextro-thyroxine and androsterone on blood clotting factors and serum cholesterol in patients with atherosclerosis," *Canadian Medical Association Journal* 85 (1961):1025–1031.

116   "cholesterol levels in patients with familial hypercholesterolemia":
J. Slack, "Risk of familial hyperlipoproteinemic states," *Lancet* (Dec. 27, 1969):1380–1382.

116   "Animal experiments in Japan found THD-341":
H. Enomoto, V. Yoshikuni, et al., "Hypocholesterolemic action of a novel delta-8 dihydroabietamide derivative, THD-341, in rats," *Atherosclerosis* 28 (1977):205–215.

117   "But when Dr. Peter T. Kuo":
P. T. Kuo, A. Wilson, J. Kostis, A. Moreyra, and R. Goldstein, "Effect of combined probucol and colestipol treatment in patients with familial hypercholesterolemia and coronary artery disease," *Chest* 86 (1984):284.

118   "The bile-acid sequestrants cholestyramine and colestipol":
A. M. Gotto, E. L. Berman, et al., "Recommendations for treatment of hyperlipidemia in adults: A joint statement of the Nutrition Committee and the Council on Arteriosclerosis," American Heart Association Special Report, *Circulation* 69 (1984):1065A–1090A.

118   "experiments at the University of Kansas Medical Center":
Medical & Pharmaceutical Information Bureau (Jun. 22, 1982).

118   "The South African Lipid Clinic of the Johannesburg Hospital":

H. C. Seftel et al., "Treatment of homozygous familial hypercholesterolemia with probucol," *South African Medical Journal* 62 (1982): 7-11.

118   "Researchers from the University of Chicago":
L. Cohen, J. Morgan, G. Woodbury, M. Barish, "Serum cholesterol in
human atherosclerotic disease: reduction by 50% with niacin and probucol
using individualized drug therapy," *Federation Proceedings* 44 (1985): 1498.

119   "Type III hyperlipoproteinemia":
National Institutes of Health Consensus Panel, "Consensus Development
Conference Statement," Conference on Lowering Blood Cholesterol (Dec.
10-12, 1984) and "Hold the eggs and butter," cover story, *Time* (Mar. 26,
1984): 56-63.

119   "A combination of nicotinic acid and clofibrate was tested by the Coro-
nary Drug Project":
L. A. Carlson and S. Rossner, "Results of the Coronary Drug Project—
An interpretation," editorial, *Atherosclerosis* 22 (1975): 317-324.

119   "The NIH Consensus Panel has stated":
National Institutes of Health Consensus Panel, "Consensus Development
Conference Statement," Conference on lowering blood cholesterol (Dec.
10-12, 1984).

119   " 'Elevated cholesterol levels' "
A. M. Gotto, Jr., "Can the progression of atherosclerosis be halted?" *PA
Drug Update* (June 1984): 17-19.

120   "advised Dr. Antonio M. Gotto":
American Heart Association *Cardiovascular Research Report*, No. 18
(summer 1984).

120   "said Dr. Daniel Steinberg":
Medical & Pharmaceutical Information Bureau (Mar. 26, 1982).

120   "And Dr. Robert W. Wissler":
Medical & Pharmaceutical Information Bureau (Jun. 22, 1982).

120   "in Lugano, Switzerland, in October 1981, Ancel Keys":
Medical & Pharmaceutical Information Bureau (Oct. 2, 1981).

120   "said Dr. Scott M. Grundy":
American Heart Association, *Cardiovascular Research Report*, No. 18
(summer 1984).

121   "explained Harvard cardiologist Eugene Braunwald":
Claudia Wallis, "When to bypass the bypass," *Time* (Dec. 19, 1983): 64.

121   "At the Montreal Heart Institute":
L. Campeau and M. Enjalbert, "The relation of risk factors to the development of atherosclerosis in saphenous-vein bypass grafts and the progression
of disease in the native circulation," *New England Journal of Medicine* 311
(1984): 1329-1332.

121   "Dr. Carlos A. DuJovne":
Medical & Pharmaceutical Information Bureau (Jan. 31, 1985).

122   "ileal bypass":
G. M. Dobrea, R. G. Wieland, and M. W. Johnson, "The effect of rapid
weight loss due to jejunoileal bypass on total cholesterol and high-density
lipoprotein," *American Journal of Clinical Nutrition* 34 (1981): 1994-1996.

122   "Some adverse results":

M. V. Krause, L. K. Mahan, *Food, Nutrition and Diet Therapy* (Philadelphia: W. B. Saunders Company, 1984), p. 537.

PART THREE, CHAPTER 1. EATING YOUR WAY TO A HEALTHY HEART

126   "Paleolithic people, according to Emory University researchers":
        S. Boyd Eaton and M. Konner, "The paleolithic nutrition, a consideration of its nature and current implications," *New England Journal of Medicine* 312 (1985): 283–289.

128   "Years ago, the American Heart Association introduced The Prudent Diet":
        I. Bennett and M. Simon, *The Prudent Diet* (New York: Bantam Books, 1974).

128   "University of Minnesota investigators set up a product sampling test":
        T. E. Katke et al., "Perceived palatability of The Prudent Diet: Results of a dietary demonstration for physicians," *Preventive Medicine* 12 (1983): 588–594.

129   "the American Heart Association has introduced a new one-diet-in-three-phases":
        Counselling the Patient with Hyperlipidemia (American Heart Association, June 1984):6–9.

129   "A panel of the AMA suggested some time ago":
        American Medical Association Council on Food and Nutrition and National Academy of Sciences/National Research Council Food and Nutrition Board, "Diet and coronary heart disease," *Journal of the American Medical Association* 222 (1972): 1647.

130   "in the imagery of pathologist Richard Minick":
        "Hold the eggs and butter," cover story, *Time* (Mar. 26, 1984): 56–63.

130   "That . . . was the conclusion of the National Diet Heart Study":
        P. S. Remmell, M. P. Casey, R. B. McGandy, and F. J. Stare, "A dietary program to lower serum cholesterol," *Journal of the American Dietetic Association* 54 (1969): 13–19.

Index

(Page numbers in italics indicate recipes.)

High density lipoproteins (HDLs),
16; cholesterol deposits and levels of, 40; elimination of cholesterol and, 33; factors that
reduce, 34; long-lived families
and high levels of, 33–34; pro-
tein in, 32; raising levels of,
33–34, 97, 120; ratio of total
cholesterol and, 40–41; relation
to LDL level, 120; saturated fats
in diet and reduction of, 37
Hippocrates, 75
Hodges, R. E., 85
Hommus, *151–152*
Homozygous familial hypercholes-
terolemia, 118
Honolulu Health Study, 23–24
Hormones, 16, 107–108, 116
Hors d'oeuvres, 133
Hulley Report, 44, 45
Human milk fat, 38
Hunger, diet and, 85
Hyperlipidemia, tests for, 120
Hyperlipoproteinemia, 119
Hypertension, polyunsaturated fats
and, 66

Ice cream, 57
Iron, binding of, 70
Israel, 22, 26–27
Italians, hypertension among, 66

Jackson County (Michigan) program, 105
Japanese: average blood cholesterol
level among, 9, 23; cardiovascular disease among, 9, 21, 77;
diet of, 79; heart attacks among
Hawaiian-, 9, 21; mushrooms in
diet of, 77
Java, 22
Jews, Yemenite (in Israel), 22

Kark, R. M., 45
Kellogg, K., 74
Kelp, sterols from, 79
Keys, A., 9, 64, 93, 120
Kidney (as food), 59
Korea, coronary heart disease
in, 21
Korean War, atherosclerosis among
casualties in, 16
Krehl, W. H., 85
Kumin, R. A., 48
Kuntzelmen, C., 105
Kuo, P. T., 117–118

Lard, 128
Laser coronary angioplasty, 19
Lecithin cholesterol acyl trans-
ferase (LCAT), 82
Legumes: carbohydrates from, 85;
cholesterol-lowering action of,
71–72; fiber in, 70
Lentils, 71
Lentils with turkey-hot dogs, *144*
Lignin, 68, 69–70; cholesterol-
binding capacity of, 74
Linoleic acid, 36, 37, 65, 81
Linoleic acid content of selected
fats, 183
Linolenic acid, 36–37; from
linoleic acid, 65
Lipids, 31
LDL. *See* Low density lipoproteins
(LDLs)
Lipid-Arteriosclerosis Prevention
clinic (University of Kansas
Medical Center), 104
Lipids, high blood (in children),
104–105
Lipoproteins, 16, 19, 31–32; im-
portance of testing for, 104;
ratio of low- and high-density,
64; transport system for, 39. *See*